The
Hour That
Changes
the World

The
Hour That
Changes
the World

A Practical Plan for Personal Prayer

Dick Eastman

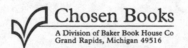

Chosen Books

A Division of Baker Book House Co
Grand Rapids, Michigan 49516

Published by Chosen Books
a division of Baker Publishing Group
P.O. Box 6287, Grand Rapids, MI 49516-6287
www.chosenbooks.com

An earlier version of this book was published by Baker Books

Printed in the United States of America

Library of Congress Cataloging-in-Publication Data
Eastman, Dick.
    The hour that changes the world : a practical plan for personal prayer / Dick Eastman.
        p.   cm.
    Includes bibliographical references.
    ISBN 10: 0-8007-9313-7 (pbk)
    ISBN 978-0-8007-9313-5 (pbk)
    1. Prayer—Christianity. 2. Twelve-step programs—Religious aspects—Christianity. I. Title.
    BV215 .E27 2002
    248.3′2—dc21   2002009042

For information concerning prayer helps mentioned in this book, the reader may contact:
Every Home for Christ
P.O. Box 6400
Colorado Springs, CO 80962
www.ehc.org
info@chc.org

23   20   19   18

To
the memory
of a wonderful friend
Jean Baumgardner
who 25 years ago
inspired the writing
of this book.

May God honor Jean's memory
with a glorious new army
of mighty praying warriors!

Contents

Contents

Before You Begin

Thoughts from Joni Eareckson Tada

It was the summer of 1984 and I was catching up with an old friend over lunch. When she asked me about my journey with the Lord Jesus, I smiled and replied, "I am convinced there's so much more to know, so much more to enjoy and understand about the Lord, and I've been asking Him to show me how to go deeper."

My friend grinned and said, "Joni, I just happen to have something that may be an answer to your prayer." She then pulled out of her handbag a copy of *The Hour That Changes the World*.

At first I was skeptical. It was such an unpretentious-looking little book. After I read it, however, I realized its insights and directives were *just* what I needed. The following week I made a copy of the page with the prayer plan, asked my husband to tape it to my bedroom wall unit, and then every night I dived into praise and waiting, confession and Scripture praying, watching, intercession, and all the rest. Little did I know that I was embarking on the most marvelous, awe-inspiring adventure of my Christian walk.

From that time on, my bed became an altar of praise. As a quadriplegic I cannot sit in my wheelchair too long, and I used to resent the early-to-bed routine. But when I began

9

to see my bed as a prayer platform, when I realized that lying down gave me a "looking-up" position (a great prayer stance!), I started to look forward to 8:30 P.M.

The hours I spent communing with the Lord Jesus catapulted me into a whole new dimension of joy in the Lord. Those hours—and many hours since—have ushered me into the deep recesses of my Savior's heart. My time of prayer became the hour that changed not only my world but the world of our mission at Joni and Friends as we strive to reach for Christ thousands of people around the globe with disabilities.

I am sure this explains why, years later, I always keep a couple of extra copies of Dick Eastman's little masterpiece on my office shelf. I do so for those occasions when my conversation with a visitor to our office turns to deeper and more personal things in life. It happened not long ago when a young college student asked, "How can I know Jesus better? How can I make a difference in the world?" Sometimes it can be a tired saint who wonders, *How can I regain my first love?*

The Hour That Changes the World may appear small and modest, but don't let its size fool you. Full of biblical insights about prayer, packed with testimonies of prayer warriors from years past, brimming with practical suggestions that will help you carve out a purposeful time of praise and intercession, Dick Eastman's book is arguably the most significant book on prayer written in modern times. It may look small, but in every way it is definitely *large*.

It is a hurting world around us, and this poor planet, splitting apart at the seams, needs prayer. From Afghanistan to Africa, hurting people need someone who will intercede for them. Even here in America—from schoolteachers to hairstylists, from grocers to gas station attendants, from policemen to the people over your backyard fence—our world is desperate for a prayerful touch. Together may we seek the Lord in prayer as to how we can fit into His strategy to reach for Christ those who are helpless and hopeless. And in so doing may we discover that our hours in praise, confession, and intercession change not only the world beyond us . . . but *our* world, too.

Joni Eareckson Tada
Agoura Hills, California

A Quarter-Century of Blessing

Thoughts from the Author

I grew up singing the old hymn "Draw Me Nearer," and particularly recall the stanza that begins "O the pure delight of a single hour that before Thy throne I spend." Yet it was not until my early thirties that I discovered how this delight could touch every day that I lived, in a practical way. That discovery changed my prayer life.

Moved by Christ's appeal to Peter in Matthew 26:40, "Could you not watch with Me one hour?" (NKJV), I embarked on a journey of blessing that has touched every day since.

Twenty-five years ago this simple challenge to set aside an hour a day to be with the Lord, in His Word, was born. It resulted from those early days of seeking to develop a consistent, daily, devotional hour. Because of a special burden for world evangelization, my hour included a plan to pray for the nations each day, thus becoming a daily hour that let me partner with God in changing our world.

It is with my deep gratitude to the Lord for His blessing that this special twenty-fifth anniversary edition of *The Hour That Changes the World* is being published. I have been encouraged that some fifty printings of this book have been released in numerous languages over these twenty-five years.

I believe God is raising up an entirely new generation of faithful, fervent warriors of worship and intercession who will truly change our world through their prayers. If they are like me when I started out, they will appreciate a few guidelines to help them begin—and to stay faithful. I pray these pages will help.

In addition to the hundreds of thousands who have read this simple book, the circle of prayer, central to this study (with twelve prayer focuses of five minutes each), has been reprinted in magazines, newsletters, prayer guides, and church bulletins. It has also been photocopied all over the world, often presented to groups with accompanying teaching, even in such places as Saudi Arabia, Iran, Syria, Jordan, and Cuba. This training has touched people of various languages, including Chinese, Russian, Arabic, Swahili, Lingala, Farsi, Hindi, Indonesian, Tagalog, Nepalese, Burmese, Thai, Korean, and Vietnamese, as well as more familiar languages like German, French, Spanish, Portuguese, and Italian (to name only several).

Now the book is becoming a helpful tool for those joining continuous "Walls of Prayer." In churches and communities, believers are commiting at least one different hour a week in prayer to fill all 168 hours with nonstop praying. (I explain this concept more fully in chapter 14 of this special edition.)

It seems that God is clearly calling His people everywhere to prayer, and as Matthew Henry said generations ago, "Whenever God is preparing to do something great in the earth, He first sets His people a-praying!" Truly something great from God must be at hand! The Church is certainly praying as never before.

I am particularly grateful to Baker Book House for first publishing this challenge 25 years ago and to Chosen Books for releasing this special 25th anniversary edition. Most of all, I am grateful to God for the many people I have run into over the years—like Joni Eareckson Tada, who kindly shares her testimony in the foreword—who have experienced how these biblical steps of prayer have helped them get started and keep going in daily prayer.

For me, I cannot imagine a day without the worship and wonder of waiting on God's presence for a single hour. I invite you to share in this joy. It could change your life, and your world as well. I'm convinced it will make your day!

Dick Eastman
International President
Every Home for Christ

1

Prayer

The Slender Nerve of Power

"Oh! One hour with God infinitely exceeds all the plea-sures and delights of this lower world.
                                    David Brainerd (1718–1747)

Prayer is the divine enigma—that marvelous mystery hidden behind the cloud of God's omnipotence. Nothing is beyond the reach of prayer because God Himself is the focus of prayer. E. M. Bounds agreed when he wrote, "Prayer is the contact of a living soul with God. In prayer, God stoops to kiss man, to bless man, and to aid in everything that God can devise or man can need."[1] Charles Spurgeon adds, "Prayer is the slender nerve that moveth the muscles of omnipotence."[2]

Prayer! What exactly is it? Basically, prayer is the simplest act a creature of God can perform. It is divine communion with our heavenly Father. Prayer does not require advanced education. Knowledge is not a prerequisite to engage in it. Only an act of the will is required to pray.

But prayer is more. Prayer is the vision of the believer. It gives eyes to our faith. In prayer we see beyond ourselves and focus spiritual eyes on God's infinite power.

Prayer is also man's ultimate indication of trust in his heavenly Father. Only in prayer do we surrender our problems completely to God and ask for divine intervention.

But, sadly, few make prayer a part of their daily experience. They pray only if extra time is available or if their emotions draw them to prayer. Oh, that Christians would see prayer in its proper perspective!

Prayer is not optional. On the contrary, it is quite obligatory. Where there is an absence of prayer there will be an absence of power. Where there is frequency of prayer there will be a continuing display of God's power. God said, "If my people, which are called by my name, shall humble themselves, and pray, and seek my face, and turn from their wicked ways; then will I hear from heaven, and will forgive their sin, and will heal their land" (2 Chron. 7:14).

The Searching Instinct

But where do we begin in our quest for spiritual power? We need only follow the instinct of the heart to pray. This searching instinct fills the human spirit. The moment we turn to Christ it comes alive. We suddenly yearn to fellowship with the Father. As Charles Spurgeon said, "To seek aid in time of distress from a supernatural Being is an instinct of human nature. I believe in the truthfulness of this instinct, and that man prays because there is something in prayer. As when the Creator gives His creature the power of thirst, it is because water exists to meet its thirst; and as when He creates hunger there is food to correspond to the appetite; so when He inclines men to pray it is because prayer has a corresponding blessing connected with it."[3]

This prayer instinct is somewhat difficult to understand and to explain. Somehow, the simple act of prayer links a sovereign God to a finite man. When man prays, God responds. Difficult situations change. Unexplained miracles occur.

But when we neglect the closet of prayer we remove ourselves from the focus of God's power. Dr. E. Stanley Jones explains, "In prayer you align yourselves to the purpose and power of God and He is able to do things through you that He couldn't do otherwise. For this is an open universe, where some things are left open, contingent upon our doing them. If we do not do them, they will never be done. For God has left certain things open to prayer—things which will never be done except as we pray."[4]

Men of Prayer

Look again at the lives of God's warriors from past generations. What qualified men like Wesley, Luther, Finney, or Brainerd for their high calling in Christ? J. C. Ryle, the nineteenth-century Bishop of Liverpool, provides a worthy answer: "I have read the lives of many eminent Christians who have been on earth since the Bible days. Some of them, I see, were rich, and some poor. Some were learned, some unlearned. Some of them were Episcopalians, and some Christians of other denominations. Some were Calvinists, and some were Arminians. Some have loved to use a liturgy, and some chose to use none. But one thing, I see, they all had in common. They all have been men of prayer."[5]

No matter our position in life or natural abilities, to be mightily used of God we must first understand a fundamental principle of spiritual power. What we do for the Lord is entirely dependent upon what we are in the Lord. Further, what we are in the Lord wholly depends upon what we receive from the Lord. And what we receive from the Lord is directly proportional to the time we spend alone with the Lord in prayer.

To spend little time with Jesus is to accomplish little in Jesus. Simply stated, there is no *true* spiritual growth apart from the devotional habit. Consistency in prayer is the evidence of true commitment. As David Hubbard shares, "Our prayer expresses our commitment to Christ. By talking to God we affirm our basic decision to depend on Him."[6]

If I seldom talk with God, it indicates He plays a secondary role in my life. Soon the world commands more of my attention than does God. Adam Clarke warns, "Apostasy begins in the closet. No man ever backslid from the life and power of Christianity who continued constant and fervent in private prayer. He who prays without ceasing is likely to rejoice evermore."[7]

The Gift of Time

Once we determine that prayer is important, our spiritual battles begin. Professor Hallesby explains in his classic book *Prayer*, "The first and decisive battle in conjunction with prayer is the conflict which arises when we are to make arrangements to be alone with God every day."[8]

The moment we determine to pray daily, Satan fills our path with distracting hindrances. Job responsibilities increase. The children demand more time. It seems we are more weary than usual.

As Dr. Hallesby further suggests, "The carnal mind will always instinctively and automatically mobilize every possible reason it can possibly conceive for not praying at a particular time. For example, you are too busy; your mind is too preoccupied; your heart is not inclined toward prayer; later on you will have more time, your mind will be more calm and collected, and you will be able to pray in a more devotional frame of mind. Before we know it, the entire day is gone, and we have not had a single quiet hour alone with Christ."[9]

Carefully mark this in your mind: *It is possible to make time for prayer!* Consider Susanna Wesley. The mother of nineteen children, including John and Charles, Susanna Wesley still found time to pray daily. This godly saint seldom gave the Lord less than a full hour each day for prayer.

"But I have no place to get away for prayer!" some might object. Susanna Wesley, likewise, had no specific place for prayer. So, at her chosen time for spiritual exercise she would take her apron and pull it over her face. Her children were instructed never to disturb "mother" when she was praying in her apron.

Like Susanna Wesley we must *make* time for prayer every day. Until we do, prayer will never become the force God intends it to be in our daily walk. Only as we apply our knowledge of prayer to the actual practice of prayer will we discover the practical power of prayer.

Fletcher of Madeley, a fellow worker with John Wesley, illustrates the importance of making prayer practical. This dedicated warrior had a most unusual conclusion to many of his lectures. Often, after discussing themes on prayer and spiritual growth, Fletcher would say to his students, "That is the theory; now will those who want the practice come along up to my room!"

Often all of Fletcher's students would quietly follow this godly saint to his room for one or two hours of actual practice in the art of prayer. They knew the secret was in "doing," not merely in "knowing."

Prayer is much more than mere theoretical power—it is practical power. But to tap this practical power we must willingly sacrifice much time. Samuel Chadwick cautions, "In these days there is not time to pray; but without time, and a lot of it, we shall never learn to pray. It ought to be possible to give God one hour out of twenty-four all to Himself."[10]

A Pattern for Praying

To be effective our sixty minutes with God should be carefully arranged. Systematic prayer adds health to the devotional habit. It helps us get started and keeps us going. Most tasks in life are accomplished systematically. In fact, without a systematic approach to life, many goals would remain unreached.

The same is true with prayer. The devotional exercise needs careful planning and preparation to function properly. Harold Lindsell cautions, "Prayer does not come naturally to men. It must be learned. Learning to pray . . . includes knowledge of the laws governing prayer as well as experience gained in the practice of prayer. Prayer must be nourished and cultivated if it is to grow."[11]

Scripture is filled with numerous concepts related to prayer that should form the basis of the devotional habit. *The Hour That Changes the World* is an attempt to present these major elements so each may be applied systematically, on a daily basis.

Although each element is clearly based on Scripture, the particular order in which they are employed may vary. To spend five minutes on each of the twelve aspects of prayer will take exactly one hour. However, some prayer warriors may desire to spend more time on certain elements than others. On occasion only eight or nine of the twelve elements may be included during your devotional hour.

Especially be careful not to become a slave to any "prayer system." Indeed, prayer is not a system at all but the development of a relationship between man and God. The highest goal of the devotional habit is to strengthen this relationship.

Prayer Works

When the question surfaces, "Why pray?" a twofold answer must be our response. First, because *Jesus calls us to prayer.* Secondly, because *prayer works.*

How well the author recalls the impact of a personal experience concerning the first reason for engaging in daily prayer. I had always believed God answers prayer, but my prayer life was never consistent. During a devotional transformation, I was gripped with the realization that Jesus asked His disciples only one question specifically related to the subject of prayer. During His intense experience in Gethsemane, Christ approached His sleeping disciples. Speaking first to Peter, Jesus asked, "Could you not watch with Me one hour?" (Matt. 26:40 NKJV).

Suddenly I realized Jesus was speaking to *me.* I, too, was a follower of Jesus. I was being challenged to make a daily sacrifice of at least one hour of my time specifically for prayer. It was my choice. No one would force me. I could either sleep or pray. I chose the latter—a decision I shall never regret. Although the battles have sometimes been difficult, the victories have always been sweet.

But there is a second reason why daily prayer is profitable. *Prayer works!* Dr. Walter Judd, missionary to China, frequently enjoyed sharing his prayer experiences from missionary days. Of these experiences the doctor related, "There would come into my spirit something that supported and helped steady me, gave me confidence and assurance during the day. I can't explain it. I can't explain how some of the food I ate tonight for supper becomes brain, some blood, some bone, but I haven't stopped eating just because I can't explain it! In the same way, I can't explain this. It is not in the realm of explanation yet, or of logical proof. It *is* in the realm of demonstration; prayer works."[12]

America's Attorney General, John Ashcroft, visited President George W. Bush several weeks after the tragic events of September 11, 2001. With him was a long-time friend. The friend told the President, "My mother is ninety years old and she prays for you every day."

A tear came to the eyes of the President as he took the man by his arm. "You tell your dear mother two things for me: First, it's working. Second, don't stop!"

From the first pages of Genesis to the last words of Revelation we see scriptural evidence that God answers prayer. Bishop J. C. Ryle adds these insights: "Prayer has obtained things that seemed impossible and out of reach. It has won victories over fire, air, earth and water. Prayer opened the Red Sea. Prayer brought water from the rock and bread from Heaven. Prayer made the sun stand still. Prayer brought fire from the sky on Elijah's sacrifice. Prayer overthrew the army of Sennacherib. Prayer has healed the sick. Prayer has raised the dead. Prayer has procured the conversion of countless souls."[13]

Indeed, all of God's Word makes it clear that nothing lies beyond the potential of prayer. But a key question awaits all who claim Christ as King: Are we ready to tap into prayer's potential by making this devotional discipline a passionate daily priority?

Accepting the Challenge

Would you consider giving God a daily, sacrificial gift of time? Not just a few spare minutes here or there, but a substantial gift—perhaps even as much as sixty minutes every day? It would be time spent alone with God in personal worship, prayer, and the reading of His Word.

Before you cry "Impossible!" and toss this book aside, please turn to page 27 and look briefly at the diagram. It shows a basic, workable plan for daily prayer.

This plan is designed to place special emphasis on affecting the world we live in through various aspects of prayer.

When properly focused, prayer does more than just change one's life. Prayer reaches out in love to our neighbors and the nations and says, "I care!"

"But why set one hour daily as my goal?"

The most reasonable answer, as stated earlier, is that Jesus used this time frame. It was in a lonely garden under a heavy Judean sky that Jesus pleaded with His disciples, "Could you not watch with Me one hour?" (Matt. 26:40 NKJV).

Our Lord knew that prayer is the only answer to our daily confrontations with the enemy. This is why, when reading the gospels, we constantly find Jesus praying. He prayed among the hypocrites in the temple, in crowds, on hillsides cluttered with disciples, in a crowded upper room, and alone on mountains outside Jerusalem. Prayer was more than a part of Christ's life, it *was* His life.

Sometimes Jesus spent whole nights praying. In His moment of greatest need, He asked His disciples to watch with Him for just one hour; but it was night and the temptation for sleep was too great. The sheep were sleeping and the Shepherd had to wage His war alone!

"But how can anyone possibly pray an entire hour?" is another recurring question. It was a question I, too, had to answer from the moment I determined to personally accept Christ's call to "watch" with Him daily for at least one hour.

Seeking an answer, I brought the matter before God in prayer. After all, if prayer really works in the first place, then to pray a prayer concerning "how to pray" ought to be the first order of business.

God answered my petition with a simple plan. He drew my attention to Paul's words spoken to Ephesian believers: "Pray . . . with all kinds of prayers (Eph. 6:18 NIV). The Amplified New Testament translates this phrase, "Pray with all [manner of] prayer and entreaty." Based on those words, the Lord showed me how to structure my devotional hour into twelve scripturally based aspects. Since I started using the plan it has seemed impossible to miss keeping this daily prayer appointment. My devotional exercise became the delight of my day. On occasion the time allotted to each aspect of prayer has expanded quite by accident, transforming an hour into a whole day. It is difficult to explain fully, but the delight steadily increases, even after 25 years.

To begin using this simple plan you can divide your hour into twelve five-minute "points of focus." This allows a specific amount of time for each aspect of prayer. (If an hour seems too lofty a goal—start with twelve minutes. Spend one minute in each of the twelve areas.) At times some areas may require only a few moments, while others—like interceding for lost souls—may require far more than five minutes. In other cases you may omit or combine some of the areas.

This plan will also help "watchmen warriors" develop a meaningful hour of prayer, whether daily or weekly, as they help fill a continuous wall of prayer each week for their city or community—a concept I explain further in chapter 14.

Regardless of how you apply these prayer elements, you will most certainly find them fresh and exciting. And think of the impact this daily gift of sixty minutes will have on our troubled world. One hour each day for an entire year equals 365 hours, or 45 continuous "eight-hour" days. Imagine asking your employer for six weeks off work next year so you can spend the time with Jesus praying for the world. That's the power of giving God just sixty minutes a day (when projected for a full year).

So, let us go forth in joyful anticipation to discover new secrets of "world-changing" prayer. Soon we shall sing with fresh excitement:

> Oh, the pure delight of a single hour
> That before Thy throne I spend,
> When I kneel in prayer
> And with Thee, Oh, God,
> I commune as friend with Friend.

To help us begin this journey to the joy of daily intimacy with God, let us ask with fresh confidence.
Lord, teach me to pray!

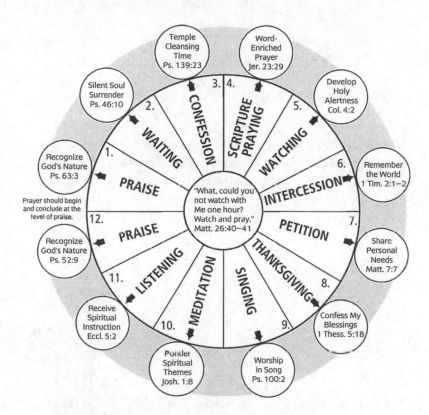

IMPORTANT: The twelve-step prayer plan in this book should be applied with spiritual liberty rather than regimented legality. After using these steps for several days or weeks, allow your own prayer program to develop.

2

Praise

The Act of Divine Adoration

J esus left His disciples but a single prayer as an example upon which to base their praying. Although several of Christ's prayers are recorded in Scripture, only once did He

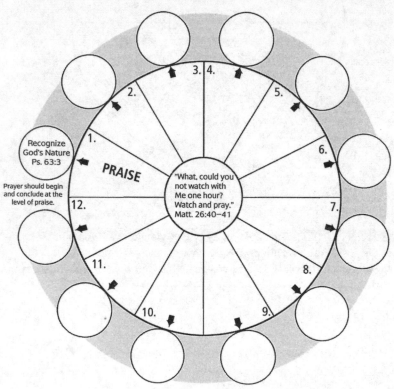

Recognize
God's Nature
Ps. 63:3

Prayer should begin
and conclude at the
level of praise.

PRAISE

"What, could you
not watch with
Me one hour?
Watch and pray."
Matt. 26:40–41

1. 2. 3. 4. 5. 6. 7. 8. 9. 10. 11. 12.

say, "After this manner therefore pray ye." The prayer is recorded in its entirety in Matthew 6:9–13 and appears somewhat abbreviated in Luke 11:2–4. It is commonly called The Lord's Prayer, although The Disciples' Prayer would be a more accurate label. The first ten words of this important prayer provide the believer with a biblical foundation for commencing all prayer with a season of praise. The prayer begins, "Our Father which art in heaven, Hallowed be thy name" (Matt. 6:9).

The goal of all praying is summed up in the expression "Hallowed be thy name." *Hallowed* is a New Testament expression used only in reference to the name of God. The Greek word for our word *hallow* is *hagiazo*, meaning "to revere or to sanctify." Since *sanctify* means "to set apart," our prayer time should include several moments, at the very outset, when God's name is set apart strictly as the object of our divine worship. During these moments of praise our sole purpose is to bring glory to God with our words. God declared through the psalmist, "Whoso offereth praise glorifieth me" (Ps. 50:23).

The Chief End

Praise is more than a single aspect of prayer. Praise is a way of life. The Westminster Catechism explains, "The chief end of man is to glorify God and to enjoy Him forever." Praise helps the believer achieve this "chief end." In fact, praise might well *be* the "chief end."

Brother Lawrence, a sixteenth-century monk, accurately summarized this thought when he wrote, "The end we ought to propose to ourselves is to become, in this life, the most perfect worshipers of God we can possibly be, as we hope to be through all eternity."[1]

What is praise? First, praise is the vocal adoration of God. Adoration is the act of rendering divine honor, esteem, and love. The word *adoration* is derived from an ancient expression that meant "to apply the hand to the mouth," or "to kiss the hand." In certain countries a kiss of the hand is still a symbol of deep respect and submission.

The act of vocal adoration is important because it implies we acknowledge God as God. Harold Lindsell explains, "Since adoration brings man into immediate and direct contact with God, in the role of servant to Master, or the created to the Creator, it is foundational to all other kinds of prayer."[2]

Why Praise First?

Aside from the fact that Jesus listed praise first in His prayer, there are numerous reasons for placing it first when we pray. Only praise puts God in His rightful position at the very outset of our praying. In praising God we declare His sovereignty and recognize His nature and power.

Some have taught that confession should be first in prayer because sin makes effective praying impossible. True, sin does rob prayer of power. And confession is important. But were it not for a loving, merciful God, confession of sins would mean very little, regardless of when it was included during prayer. So, we must first draw our attention to God in prayer before we draw our attention to self.

Another major reason for offering praise early in prayer is the fact that, in its very nature, praise is unselfish. Paul Billheimer relates, "Here is one of the greatest values of praise: it decentralizes self. The worship and praise of God demands a shift of center from self to God. One cannot praise God without relinquishing occupation with self. Praise produces forgetfulness of self—and forgetfulness of self is health."[3]

We soon discover spiritual health has its roots in divine adoration. Thus, praise is quite practical. It is practical because it changes our focus. As the believer recognizes God for all He is, he soon realizes it is this all-powerful God to whom he will be presenting all of his later petitions.

The Voice of Praise

Offering praise at the outset of prayer is also wise because of the biblical precedent given to praise. Praise sparks victory. Note the scriptural account of God's glory flooding His earthly temple: "It came even to pass, as the trumpeters and singers were as one, to make one sound to be heard in praising and thanking the LORD . . . that then the house was filled with a cloud, even the house of the LORD; So that the priests could not stand to minister by reason of the cloud: for the glory of the LORD had filled the house of God" (2 Chron. 5:13–14).

Preaching on this passage, Dwight L. Moody said, "Solomon prevailed much with God in prayer at the dedication of the temple, but it was the voice of praise which brought down the glory that filled the house."[4]

Not only does praise open our devotional hour to an outpouring of God's glory, but it promptly sends Satan running. He cannot tolerate the presence of God.

Where do we find God's presence? In Psalm 22:3 we are reminded that God inhabits "the praises" of His people. God manifests His living presence in the praise-saturated chamber of prayer. Adoration is the antidote to the poison of satanic oppression. To develop the "praise-life" is to develop a certain immunity to the enemy's attacks. Paul Billheimer further suggests, "Satan is allergic to praise, so where there is massive triumphant praise, Satan is paralyzed, bound, and banished."[5]

Our Prize Possession

"Praise the Lord" is an expression commonplace in the vocabulary of most believers. But what exactly do we mean when we say, "Praise the Lord"? Basically, praise is the act of expressing one's esteem of a person for his virtues or accomplishments. It is to pronounce that person "worthy of honor."

But rendering praise to God is even more. The full meaning of praise can be captured only in its Old French origin, *preiser*, which means "to prize"! To *praise* God is to *prize* God. The word *prize* means "to value, esteem, and cherish something." During our times of praise we cherish and esteem God with our words of adoration.

Prize also means "to estimate the worth of." In "praise" we mentally gather together all the facts we know about God and we put these facts into words. Praise literally becomes "the fruit of our lips" unto God (Heb. 13:15).

Because praise is to verbalize our esteem for God, it seems unlikely we will exhaust any potential list of possibilities for praise. The following are but a few scriptural suggestions for your moments of ministering unto the Lord through praise.

First, we should *praise God for His name*. The psalmist said, "Not unto us, O LORD, not unto us, but unto thy name give glory" (Ps. 115:1). Although various titles describing God are shared throughout the Old Testament, the actual "name of the Lord" is not specifically revealed until the pages of the New Testament. His "name" is *the Lord Jesus Christ*.

It greatly honors God when we take time during prayer to "prize" the name of Jesus Christ with words of praise. A veteran Bible teacher once declared, "If you want to get in good with God, just brag on His Son."

When praising the name of Jesus in prayer we may use expressions from Scripture, such as those used by Isaiah:

"And his name shall be called Wonderful, Counsellor, The mighty God, The everlasting Father, The Prince of Peace" (Isa. 9:6).

Secondly, we should *praise God for His righteousness.* All that God is deserves our praise. The psalmist intoned, "And my tongue shall speak of thy righteousness and of thy praise all the day long" (Ps. 35:28).

Righteous means "meeting the standards of what is right and just." God does more than meet certain standards; *God is the standard.* All that a prayer warrior can imagine concerning God's faithfulness, justice, and mercy may become a theme for these moments of praise.

Thirdly, we should *praise God for His infinite creation.* The psalmist said succinctly, "Praise him for his mighty acts" (Ps. 150:2).

Because we are challenged to praise God for His "mighty acts," there is no limit to praise. God created countless species of plant and animal life, each serving as an individual basis for praise. The scope of praise ranges from the microscopic particles of the atom to the spiraling galaxies of the universe. All of creation is a treasure house of praise.

Finally, we should *praise God for His Word.* During moments of deep depression King David wrote, "In God will I praise his word" (Ps. 56:10).

How do we praise the Word of God? The answer is revealed in Psalm 19. Note this excellent outline for praising God's Word. We may offer praise because . . .

1. "The law of the LORD is perfect, converting the soul."
2. "The testimony of the LORD is sure, making wise the simple."
3. "The statutes of the LORD are right, rejoicing the heart."
4. "The commandment of the LORD is pure, enlightening the eyes."
5. "The fear of the LORD is clean, enduring forever."

6. "The judgments of the LORD are true and righteous altogether."

Truly, the possibilities for praise stretch beyond the limits of our imagination. Because God has no limit, our praise is limitless.

Early in prayer take time to recognize all that God is. Express these thoughts vocally. And don't be in a hurry to go beyond praise until you have taken adequate time to adore God with your words of worship.

Lord, teach me to adore you!

Praise: The First Step in World-Changing Prayer

1. Sanctify, or set aside, a period of time specifically to praise God at the beginning of your prayer.
2. Select a specific theme for praise, such as God's righteousness, His Word, or His creative acts.
3. Drawing on your selected theme, declare vocally all that God is.
4. Expand your theme as much as possible. Allow God to reveal new themes for worship as your time of praise develops.

3

Waiting
The Act of Soul Surrender

F ew saints have longed after God with such sincerity as
  did Madame Guyon. Early in life, seeking spiritual
encouragement, she approached a devout Franciscan friar.

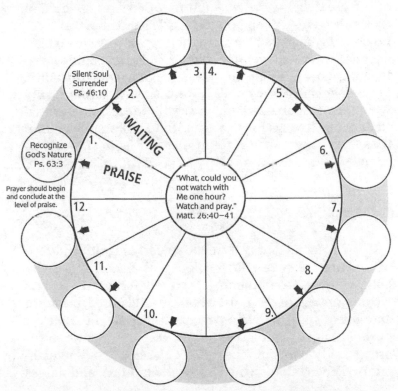

The young woman explained her desire for God had grown shamefully weak.

After hearing her story the friar engaged in silent contemplation for a considerable time. Slowly the old Franciscan gazed up at Madame Guyon and declared, "Your efforts have been unsuccessful, because you have *sought without* only what you can *find within*. Accustom yourself to seek God in your heart, and you will not fail to find Him."[1]

Madame Guyon had received her introduction to a most vital element of prayer, that of silently waiting in the presence of God. All who would be used of God must learn this secret of silence. In her classic study, *Creative Prayer*, Bridgid E. Herman explained, "If we read the biographies of the great and wise, we shall find they were people of long silences and deep ponderings. Whatever of vision, of power, of genius there was in their work was wrought in silence. And when we turn to the inner circle of the spiritual masters—the men and women, not necessarily gifted or distinguished, to whom God was a living, bright reality which supernaturalized their everyday life and transmuted their homeliest actions into sublime worship—we find that their roots struck deep into the soil of spiritual silence."[2]

A Dose of Silence

To be complete, prayer needs an early, significant dose of spiritual silence. Such silence is necessary if the believer hopes to minister effectively for Jesus. Just as virtue went out of our Lord when He ministered, a certain amount of spiritual virtue seems to depart the believer during his daily ministry (see Luke 8:46). A student of prayer said, "We cannot be made a blessing to others without perceiving that virtue has gone out of us, and unless this is constantly renewed with loving communion with Heaven, our service becomes little more than dead works, and our message loses the ring which bespeaks its divine origin."[3]

J. Gregory Mantle says, "Work is not food for the spirit any more than for the body. Amidst a multitude of works the worker's soul may wither, and his activities will prove this in due time."[4]

What does it mean to "wait" upon God? And how does waiting differ from praise? Scripture includes numerous insights into the ministry of waiting: "I will wait on thy name" (Ps. 52:9). "My soul waiteth upon God" (Ps. 62:1). "My soul waiteth for the Lord more than they that watch for the morning" (Ps. 130:6). "They that wait upon the LORD shall renew their strength" (Isa. 40:31).

Waiting on the Lord is basically the silent surrendering of the soul to God. John Bisagno observed, "Waiting upon God requires our entire being. It is not drifting into daydreaming, but is rather an exercise that demands our keenest attention, our most alert frame of mind and all of our soul's attention to the Heavenly Voice."[5]

Waiting is not praise, though it is closely related to praise and flows directly from it. Praise is verbalizing our esteem of God. Waiting is a time of silent love. Praise cries boldly, "God, I see these excellent qualities in your nature." Waiting says softly, "God, I love you."

A Spiritual Love Affair

The act of waiting is well illustrated by the experience of an elderly saint. One day an acquaintance asked her how she usually spent her days.

The lady quickly replied, "Well, I always begin my day with a good season of prayer. In fact, I pray until I can't pray any more. Then I take my Bible and read until I can't read any more. After that, I take my hymnbook from the shelf and I sing until I can't sing any more. Then I just sit quietly and let God love me."

To a great degree our time of waiting might be termed "wordless worship." It is a spiritual love affair with intimate supernatural union. Professor Hallesby spoke of this intimacy as the "soul's fellowship with God in prayer." The saintly Bible teacher added, "There is something in our lives, also in our fellowship, which can never be formulated in words, which can be the common experience, nevertheless, of two who share with each other everything that can be expressed in words."[6]

The professor illustrated this intimacy with an experience from his early ministry. One day his son bumped his head in the entryway of the professor's study. The lad knew his father was not to be disturbed during these important hours of study. His conscience troubling him, the youngster quietly approached his father. Gazing tenderly with loving eyes, the lad pleaded, "Papa, dear, I will sit still all the time if you will only let me be here with you."[7]

Being alone with God is the central issue of waiting. Genuine prayer is not merely asking for things; it is a relationship. Asking is only a part of prayer, and asking must come later. Strong relationships are best cultivated in silence. My wife and I were much in love long before words could adequately express that love. Being with each other was enough.

It is also important to understand that our time of waiting is not necessarily a time of listening. Listening is crucial to prayer, but as with the aspect of asking, listening will come later. For now we simply surrender our hearts to the Lord in quiet love. In these silent moments we respond as Job: "What shall I answer thee? I will lay mine hand upon my mouth" (Job 40:4).

The Focus of Waiting

John of Damascus, the ancient Greek theologian, defined waiting as "the elevation of the mind to God."[8]

Here we find the true focus of waiting. All attention must center in our heavenly Father. We come to know the Lord only at this most intimate level. The knowledge of God is best revealed in silent waiting. Scripture declares, "Be still, and know that I am God" (Ps. 46:10).

As one author expressed, "The highest worship of almighty God consists in being wholly taken up with Him. It is the most intimate form of communion in which the creature adores his Creator, the finite before the Infinite, the powerless before the Powerful, the nothing before the All."[9]

Of course, for very practical reasons God must be the central focus of our praying. There is no power for prayer apart from God. Scripture does not say, "Have faith in prayer," but, "Have faith in God" (Mark 11:22).

Far more important than the answer to our prayer is the focus of our prayer. Donald E. Demaray accurately wrote, "The point of prayer is to get God. Answers are most meaningful when they are thought of least. Prayer is most meaningful when God is thought of most."[10]

Waiting on God is especially essential to prayer because it strengthens our knowledge and concept of God. To focus attention entirely upon God places God on the throne of our praying. Ralph Herring shares the following insight in his *The Cycle of Prayer:* "Only a sovereign God can inspire prayer, and only a sovereign God can answer it. A man's concept of God, therefore, determines the depth of his prayer life. Real prayer begins and ends with God enthroned."[11]

Remember, we were not only challenged by the psalmist to "Be still," but to "know God" as well. Knowing someone intimately is impossible with limited attention. Intimacy takes time and concentration. This is why these early moments of prayer need a careful silencing of the mind, with all thoughts directed toward the person of God alone.

The Value of Waiting

Tragically, many believers become deceived by a spirit of selfishness that often follows them directly into the closet of prayer. Waiting helps deal with this spirit. It is an important step that prepares us for our time of confession, which is next on our list of prayer elements. Bridgid Herman wrote, "The most formidable enemy of the spiritual life, and the last to be conquered, is self-deception; and if there is a better cure for self-deception than silence, it has yet to be discovered."[12]

Not only does waiting prepare the prayer warrior for *confession* in prayer, but it actually serves to snatch us away from the things of the world. To wait in silence is to bid farewell to earthly conversation and attention. It is that vital bridge that takes us from a carnal world to a spiritual world. This silent surrendering of the soul to God opens the door to the "higher plane" of His divine love.

Thoughts from Dr. Andrew Bonar illustrate this concept. Bonar, a man greatly used of God, carefully kept a diary never intended for publication. Fortunately, one of his daughters knew his code system and was able in later years to translate the diary. An especially meaningful entry reads, "Some people have got the beauty of the rose of Sharon, and there are others who have the fragrance, too. Spent two hours today in prayer, seeking that I might have the fragrance."[13]

The Divine Link

Like any worthy spiritual vocation, waiting in prayer takes time. "A great part of my time," said Robert Murray

McCheyne, "is spent in getting my heart in tune for prayer. It is the divine link that connects earth with heaven."[14]

We must not rush these moments of spiritual silence. If any quality seems typically "Christian," it is our impatience with God's timing. An unknown saint confessed, "Many a man asks in April a gift of divine fruit that will be ripe only in June."

We must wait for the best of God's blessings, even in prayer. Consider the case of Paul. When he surrendered his life to Christ, he immediately sought a mission: "Lord, what wilt thou have me to do?" (Acts 9:6). And what was God's answer? He immediately sent Paul into the solitude of a quiet Arabian desert.

A spare ten or fifteen minutes here and there, listening to the latest cassette of a noted minister, or reading a best-seller on Christian growth, will never provide the food needed for true spiritual development. Building a friend-ship takes much time. The Bible says, "And the LORD spake unto Moses *face to face*, as a man speaketh unto his friend" (Exod. 33:11, italics added).

Little wonder Moses came from the mountain with his face shining. He met God "face to face." Here was a man who waited decades in a barren wilderness before catch-ing a glimpse of the true glory of God. But, oh, the results of his lonely desert sojourn. Moses touched God, and God, in turn, touched Moses in those years of waiting.

Take Time to Wait

Concerning the importance of spiritual waiting, Andrew Murray wrote, "Here is the secret of a life of prayer. *Take time* in the inner chamber to bow down and worship; and *wait on Him* until He unveils Himself, and takes posses-sion of you, and goes out with you to show how a man can live and walk in abiding fellowship with an unseen Lord."[15]

Especially strive to conquer the spirit of misspent conversation that permeates the very fiber of human life. Practice the art of silence throughout your day. A wise writer reminds, "The one fact we forget is that the saints of old were capable of spiritual silence simply because they had not contracted our modern habit of ceaseless talk in their ordinary life. Their days were days of silence, relieved by periods of conversation, while ours are a wilderness of talk with a rare oasis of silence."[16]

Oh, that more believers would earnestly seek the power of sacred silence. Scripture declares, "Be silent, O all flesh, before the LORD: for he is raised up out of his holy habitation" (Zech. 2:13).

Strive to devote the early moments of your devotional hour to a time of silent sharing with the Lord. Wait patiently for a greater glimpse of His infinite glory. May our hearts cry out with the unknown poet,

> Oh, to see our Saviour's face!
>   From sin and sorrow to be freed!
> To dwell in His divine embrace—
>   This will be sweeter far indeed!
> The fairest form of earthly bliss
>   Is less than nought compared with this.

Lord, teach me to wait!

Waiting: The Second Step in World-Changing Prayer

1. After your moments of praise, bring your mind and spirit into a time of complete silence to the world.
2. Think no thoughts but thoughts of God the Father, His Son, Jesus, or the Holy Spirit.
3. If words are to be voiced, let them be quiet whispering like, "I love you, Lord," or, "I long for your presence, O God."
4. Concentrate full attention on the "love" aspect of God's nature in these minutes of silence.

4

Confession

The Act of Declared Admission

Having honored God with vocal praise and silent love, we find the door now opens for truly effective praying. Immediately we must deal fully with the matter of per-

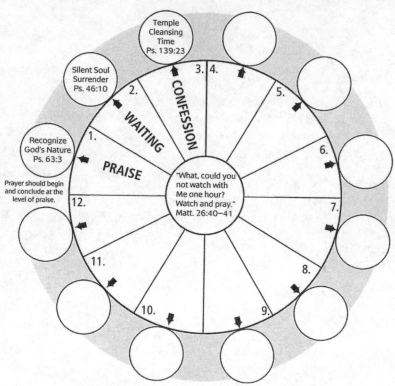

sonal sin. Andrew Murray reminds us, "God cannot hear the prayers on our lips often because the desires of our heart after the world cry out to Him much more strongly and loudly than our desires for Him."[1]

An awareness of our past failures especially tends to buffet the mind as we pray. Suddenly we feel hopelessly unworthy of offering our petitions. The devil has gained a victory and soon we stop praying altogether.

To combat these spiritual attacks we must take at face value all the promises of God concerning confession. "If we confess our sins," declared the apostle John, "He [God] is faithful and just to forgive us our sins, and to cleanse us from all unrighteousness" (1 John 1:9). If unrighteousness renders our praying ineffective, then confession is the solution to the problem of sin-guilt in prayer.

What is confession? The New Testament Greek word for *confess* means "to agree with God" concerning His opinion of a matter. It also means "to admit my guilt." When we confess our sins we are agreeing with God concerning the sin in our lives, as revealed through His Word by the Holy Spirit.

Confession is to verbalize our spiritual shortcomings and admit we have sinned. Simply stated, confession is the act of declared admission.

At no other time in prayer does the believer look so carefully at his own spiritual growth as during *confession*. Both King David and Solomon spoke of this as communing with their own hearts. Dwight L. Moody called it a "personal debate betwixt ourselves and our hearts." Defining this aspect of prayer, Moody added, "Commune—or hold a serious communication and clear intelligence and acquaintance—with your own hearts."[2]

Heartfelt Recognition

Confession is a heartfelt recognition of what we are. It is important to God because it indicates that we take seriously our mistakes and failures. Of course, God does not ask us to confess our sins because He needs to know we have sinned, but because He knows that *we* need to know we have sinned.

William R. Parker and Elaine St. Johns, psychologists who carefully studied the psychological impact of prayer, also discussed the importance of confession. According to these authors, "People should think less about what they ought to do and more about what they ought to be. If only their being were good, their works would shine forth brightly."[3]

This brings to our attention an essential law of prayer: *My prayer life will never rise above my personal life in Jesus Christ.* If my personal life touches too much of the world, my prayer life suffers. The psalmist put it succinctly, "If I regard iniquity in my heart, the LORD will not hear me" (Ps. 66:18).

According to Scripture there can be no effective prayer life where sin maintains its grip in the life of the believer. This is why confession is critical to our praying and should be implemented early in prayer. It clears the conscience of faith-killing guilt and opens the heart to truly believe God will hear our petitions.

Why is confession so difficult for some? Perhaps because confession is really the most painful part of personal prayer. The moment we admit that a particular act displeases God, we recognize the responsibility to change it. Immediately an inner battle of the will begins to take place.

Speaking of confession, E. M. Blaiklock explains, "This period of our devotions must contain a moment of pain. It is not God's intention that we should writhe under it, or linger in it. But specific and sincere confession of our own sin is no joyous exercise; and self-contempt, however salutary, is not pleasant. But let evil in conduct, thought or motive be brought into the open, fully, without excuse, and under proper names. It is of no use, after all, to pose before God."[4]

Spiritual Surgery

This act of declared admission gives God access into the heart of a believer, removing all hindrances to effective prayer. It could well be described as a spiritual work of surgery. "It [confession] works healing to the wound incurred in the heart," Harold Lindsell writes. "Just as the surgeon lances a boil to permit the infection to drain and to heal from the inside, so confession opens the sore, drains the poison, and heals from within."[5]

There can be no healing *within* until there is first confession *without*. Confession is conditional to cleansing. Until known sin is fully dealt with, we are not ready to pray. Meister Johannes Eckhart said, "God is bound to act, to pour Himself into thee as soon as He shall find thee ready."[6]

The great question confronting us at this stage of prayer is, "Am I truly ready to pray for a lost and unevangelized world?" And what about the personal needs of my family and friends? Their well-being depends upon my prayers. But my prayers depend upon *my* spiritual well-being. John Allan Lavender accurately suggests, "Before you pray for a change in circumstances, you should pray for a change in character."[7]

As Christians our ultimate goal in prayer must be to glorify God by changing the world. God desires to pour Himself through us into our world, thus bringing about this change.

Herein lies the problem. How can a holy God pour Himself through a believer whose life is clogged with the debris of this world? Sin causes indifference, and it is impossible for indifferent people to change the world. Daily we must pray as the psalmist, "Search me, O God, and know my heart: try me, and know my thoughts: And see if there be any wicked way in me, and lead me in the way everlasting" (Ps. 139:23–24).

A careful study of Scripture reveals how important confession truly is. Those most mightily used of God were also those most willing to confess their weaknesses. Only after Isaiah cried, "I am undone," did the Lord invite him to serve. When Job confessed his sins and prayed for his friends God changed his circumstances and gave him more blessings than during his greatest days of prosperity.

Daniel is another example. His life was so godly that the evil princes could find no fault in him (see Dan. 6:4). But note Daniel's awareness of personal sin. He wrote, "And whiles I was speaking, and praying, and *confessing* my sin and the sin of my people Israel, and presenting my supplication before the LORD my God for the holy mountain of my God . . . even the man Gabriel . . . touched me about the time of the evening oblation" (Dan. 9:20–21, italics added).

These godly servants of ancient days had learned an important secret of power. The Holy Spirit works best through a clean vessel, and confession begins the process of cleansing.

The Necessity of Confession

Confession is not optional to spiritual growth. Through Isaiah God told His people, "Your iniquities have separated between you and your God, and your sins have hid his face from you, that he will not hear" (Isa. 59:2).

Confession is crucial for all spiritual growth, not merely for effective prayer. It is that necessary "first step" to repentance. Before we will ever willingly turn *from* sin, we must first admit that what we are doing *is* sin.

Preaching on Pharaoh's earnest plea to Moses, "Entreat the LORD, that he may take away the frogs from me" (Exod. 8:8), Charles Spurgeon said, "A fatal flaw is manifest in Pharaoh's prayer. It contains no confession of sin. He says not, 'I have rebelled against the Lord: entreat that I may find forgiveness.' Nothing of the kind; he loves sin as much as ever."

Spurgeon concludes, "A prayer without penitence is a prayer without acceptance. If no tear has fallen upon it, it is withered. There must be confession of sin before God, or our prayer is faulty."[8]

During your times of confession especially be on guard for little things—those unseen sins that grow to cause such severe damage. Every major spiritual failure begins as a tiny seed of misconduct.

Virginia Whitman, in her excellent book *The Excitement of Answered Prayer*, tells of an incident that occurred in New York City. "Someone tossed an empty beverage can in front of a subway train just as it was entering a tunnel. It was only a tin can but somehow that can landed on the 'live' electrical rail, causing a major power failure. The result was an hour and a half delay that affected an amazing 55 trains and 75,000 passengers."[9]

The How of Confessing

The author has found a particular psalm to be of special help in establishing a pattern for daily confession. Each day during this phase of prayer I center my attention on David's confession found in Psalm 51. David prayed, "Create in me a clean heart, O God; and renew a right spirit within me. Cast me not away from thy presence; and take not thy holy spirit from me" (Ps. 51:10–11). Here David provides a practical fourfold pattern for daily confession.

First, David cries out for *divine holiness.* "Create in me a clean heart," he pleads. I cannot be cleansed or forgiven by my own actions. Forgiveness is a work only God can do. So during confession I amplify David's request, elaborating on areas that I believe need improvement in my life. I quietly ask God to show me what needs cleansing.

Often a quick mental trip through the previous twenty-four hours reveals the need for confession. Ask yourself, "Did I fail God in any areas of personal conduct?" "Was I honest in my dealings with others?" "Were my thoughts pleasant to God?" As God reveals various spiritual shortcomings, confess them and claim total victory.

Next, David cries out for a *divine attitude*. He continues, "And renew a right spirit within me."

Whereas David's first petition concerns a right relationship with God (a clean heart), this petition concerns a right relationship with others (a renewed spirit). Helen Shoemaker observes, "Unless our attitude toward others is forgiving and redemptive, God will not hear us."[10]

Mrs. Shoemaker illustrates her thought with a legend concerning the noted artist Leonardo da Vinci. According to the account, during the painting of "The Last Supper," da Vinci chose as his subject for Judas a much-hated enemy. Later, prior to the day the face of Jesus was to be painted, da Vinci was deeply troubled. All night long he tossed and turned in his sleep. Morning finally arrived and the time came to paint the figure of Christ. But, as the legend relates, when da Vinci tried to paint the picture, the Lord's face became strangely blurred.

That night the artist tossed and turned again. Suddenly he jumped from his bed and rushed to the studio. In moments he erased the likeness of the enemy from the face of Judas. Then, in a flash, Leonardo da Vinci saw the picture of Christ clearly.

One's attitude is crucial to dynamic praying. Bitterness toward others drains prayer of power. David Hubbard reminds us, "The great danger in having enemies is not what they may do to us—it is what we do to ourselves as we allow harsh, bitter, angry reactions to develop."[11]

A third quality ought to be sought during this aspect of prayer. David confessed his need for *divine guidance*. The king entreated, "Cast me not away from thy presence." Here we confess our need for God's presence throughout the day, especially to defeat temptation. In the prayer Jesus gave His disciples, He taught us to pray, "Lead us not into temptation" (Matt. 6:13). To confess my confidence that God will be with me when temptation comes helps prepare me for these attacks.

Finally, David cries out for *divine unction*. Almost desperately the king confesses his need for the Holy Spirit: "Take not thy holy spirit from me."

God certainly has no intention of removing His Spirit from obedient believers. But still this aspect of confession is important. It is a renewed affirmation that we cannot accomplish anything apart from the direct spiritual aid of the Holy Spirit. It is to admit that without God's Spirit operating in and through us all efforts will be hopelessly ineffective.

Temple Cleansing Time

To a great degree, confession in prayer is a time of spiritual cleansing. In ancient Bible days it was often necessary to clean and restore God's temple. Concerning the revival and restoration of the temple under Hezekiah, the Bible tells us, "And the priests went into the inner part of the house of the LORD, to cleanse it, and brought out all the uncleanness that they found in the temple of the LORD into the court of the house of the LORD" (2 Chron. 29:16).

Today, the dwelling place of God is not a temple of brick and mortar but the inner soul of man. Scripture declares, "What? know ye not that your body is the temple of the Holy Ghost . . . ?" (1 Cor. 6:19).

Confession is necessary to private prayer because it initiates the process of cleansing our spiritual temple. Allow enough time during prayer for a thorough cleansing.

Remember, confession in prayer is that final step that leads to confident praying.

Lord, teach me to confess!

Confession: The Third Step in World-Changing Prayer

1. Following your time of silent waiting, immediately ask God to search your heart for any unconfessed sin.
2. Mentally examine your recent activities to discover possible areas of spiritual failure that need confessing.
3. Confess any specific sins you may be guilty of, either against God or your fellow man.
4. Confess your need for specific divine guidance and supernatural unction.

5

Scripture Praying

The Act of Faith Appropriation

"There are only three classes of people in the world today," an unknown preacher confessed. "Those

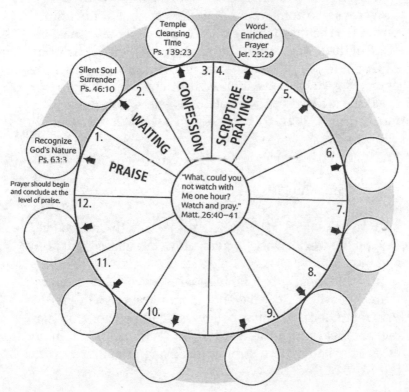

who are afraid, those who do not know enough to be afraid, and those who know their Bibles."

Although the Word of God is essential to the whole of our Christian experience, it is especially crucial to prayer. The degree to which we believe in God's Word and apply it to prayer is the degree to which God will pour out His power during our prayer.

We can never expect to grow in spiritual confidence if we spend little or no time getting to know God through His Word. Thus, God's Word must become an actual part of the devotional life. We may study the Bible throughout the week, but we should also seek to bring God's Word directly into our daily prayer.

Only as we systematically apply God's Word during prayer will we come to a full understanding of how much power God has available to us. Leonard Ravenhill preached, "One of these days some simple soul will pick up the Book of God and read it, and believe it. The rest of us will be embarrassed. We have adopted the convenient theory that the Bible is a Book to be explained, whereas first and foremost, it is a Book to be believed (and after that to be obeyed)."[1]

Divine Nourishment

"Prayer," said E. M. Bounds, "projects faith on God, and God on the world. Only God can move mountains, but faith and prayer move God."[2]

It is true that faith combined with prayer moves mountains, but where do we gain this mountain-moving faith? Paul reminded the Roman believers, "Faith cometh by hearing, and hearing by the word of God" (Rom. 10:17). In no other way is our faith strengthened as in familiarity with the Word of God.

"Fasting and long hours of prayer do not build faith," E. W. Kenyon wrote. "Reading books about faith and men of faith and their exploits stirs in the heart a deep passion for faith, but does not build faith. *The Word alone is the source of faith.*"[3]

Few writers have had as much impact on the lives of praying Christians as Andrew Murray. Like so many noted saints of God, Andrew Murray developed an intense prayer life heavily saturated with the Word of God. He once explained, "Little of the Word with little prayer is death to the spiritual life. Much of the Word with little prayer gives a sickly life. Much prayer with little of the Word gives more life, but without steadfastness. A full measure of the Word and prayer each day gives a healthy and powerful life."[4]

Our prayer time, no matter how intense, is never truly complete without the divine nourishment available only from God's Word. Indeed, the Word of God is the Christian's true prayer book. It is our guide and foundation for all effective praying. To neglect God's Word is to neglect God's power. Lehman Strauss adds, "When we neglect the daily, quiet, meditative reading of God's Word, we block the lifeline to God's throne of grace. Our abiding in Christ through the Word is a life process that must never cease."[5]

G. Campbell Morgan was another gifted minister who considered his devotional hour useless without a good helping of God's Word. The preacher cautioned, "My brothers, see to it that when morning breaks you go to God for sustenance for your spiritual life. That will make you strong against the allurements of the Devil. So many people turn out to face the temptations of the day spiritually unfed, spiritually hungry, and therefore they are attacked by all kinds of enticements of the enemy. It is the man fed by God, spiritually and physically, who is likely to overcome in the hour of temptation."[6]

Pleading God's Promises

Few leaders of the nineteenth century were known as much for their deep confidence in God and effectiveness in prayer as was George Mueller. At ninety years of age Mueller was able to declare, "I have never had an unanswered prayer." He claimed the secret to receiving answers to prayer lies in how the Christian applies God's Word during prayer.

For example, George Mueller always prayed with an open Bible. He constantly filled his petitions with God's Word. Friends said the orphanage leader would not voice a petition without a "word from God" to back that petition. In fact, Mueller never started petitioning God until *after* he nourished himself in God's Word.

Describing his devotional hour, George Mueller wrote, "The first thing I did, after having asked in a few words the Lord's blessing upon His precious Word, was to begin to meditate on the Word of God, searching as it were into every verse to get a blessing out of it; not for the sake of the public ministry of the Word, nor for the sake of preaching on what I meditated upon, but for the sake of obtaining food for my own soul. The result I have found to be almost invariably this, that after a very few minutes my soul has been led to confession, or to thanksgiving, or to intercession, or to supplication; so that, though I did not, as it were, give myself to prayer, but to meditation, yet it turned almost immediately more or less into prayer."[7]

George Mueller had learned the important secret of transforming God's Word into faith-filled petitions. He literally "prayed" the Word of God.

Charles Spurgeon was another noted leader who understood this secret. He expressed, "Every promise of Scripture is a writing of God, which may be pleaded before Him with this reasonable request, 'Do as Thou hast said!' The Creator will not cheat the creature who depends upon His truth; and far more, the Heavenly Father will not break His Word to His own child."[8]

Word-Enriched Prayer

The Word of God is more than a mere foundation for effective praying; it is the actual substance for effective praying. Just as the Word of God brings life to the believer's daily walk, God's Word brings life into our praying.

Concerning the power of Scripture, Paul declared, "For this cause also thank we God without ceasing, because, when ye received the word of God which ye heard of us, ye received it not as the word of men, but as it is in truth, the word of God, which *effectually worketh* also in you that believe" (1 Thess. 2:13, italics added). Another translation declares that God's Word has "living power in you who have faith" *(The New Testament in Basic English)*.

Years ago I discovered the amazing secret of prayer called "Scripture Praying." In Paul's words to the Thessalonians we find the basis for this mode of praying. If God's Word "effectually worketh" in those who believe, it should carry the same impact *within our prayers*. By bringing God's Word directly into our praying, we are bringing God's power directly into our praying.

The psalmist said, "I will never forget thy precepts: for *with them thou hast quickened me*" (Ps. 119:93, italics added). Note God's promise given through Jeremiah: "Is not my word like as a fire? saith the LORD; and like a hammer that breaketh the rock in pieces?" (Jer. 23:29).

E. M. Bounds was a saint of God known for his extraordinary prayer life. A lawyer during the Civil War, Bounds spent an average of four hours in prayer every morning. Immediately following prayer he would write his most intimate prayer experiences. Like other spiritual leaders of his generation, Bounds discovered the tremendous value of applying God's Word to prayer. He once testified, "The Word of God is the fulcrum (support) upon which the lever of prayer is placed, and by which things are mightily moved. God has committed Himself, His purpose, and His promise to prayer. His Word becomes the basis, the inspiration of our praying, and there are circumstances under which by importunate prayer, we may obtain an addition or an enlargement of His promises."[9]

The Method of Scripture Praying

My experiences with Scripture Praying began with a Christmas gift of Bible cassettes. Daily I would listen to passages from Psalms and Proverbs during my hour of prayer. As in the case of George Mueller, I quickly discovered that certain passages of Scripture prompted me to pray for specific needs. Before long I found that a definite plan for enriching my prayer with God's Word was developing.

Although I now simply use an open Bible in my daily devotional hour, systematically praying through Scripture a few chapters each day, you might find listening to CDs or cassettes helpful. (They are usually available at Christian bookstores.)

Following is a simple three-step plan for Scripture Praying that emerged in my daily program.

First, read (or listen to) a passage from God's Word. Try to include approximately *one chapter during each devotional hour.* Of course, you may focus on more than one chapter, but too lengthy a portion of Scripture may dilute the impact of Scripture Praying.

Remember, in using this method of praying you are not actually studying the Bible for the sake of Bible study, but you are searching the Scripture for actual power that might be applied to your petitions.

Second, while reading Scripture allow your finger to move slowly from verse to verse. The moment you discover a verse (or two) that impresses a particular truth upon your heart, *quietly meditate on what that verse is saying to you.* Ponder every aspect of this passage. This will usually happen in a matter of a few seconds. Carefully evaluate how the passage might be transformed into a specific petition. (If you're listening to a CD or cassette just push the pause button.)

Ask yourself several questions. Does this verse prompt me to pray for something specific? How can this passage be directly applied to my petition? Is it possible to use some of the words of this scripture, verbatim, as I pray?

Third, with these moments of meditation as a base, *form a personal prayer "enriched" by that promise from God.* In some cases you may read (or listen) to an entire chapter before receiving a specific thought that will directly apply to a particular petition. But when that thought comes, use it to enhance your request. Mentally develop an actual prayer based on what you have read (or heard) in the passage and offer that prayer to the Lord.

As you develop this method of praying, keep in mind that it is not necessary to form a prayer for every verse of a chapter. In fact, some passages of Scripture are somewhat difficult to use in Scripture Praying. For the most part, Psalms, Proverbs, the Gospels, or Epistles provide the best setting for this method of praying.

Beyond Word-enriched prayer the intercessor will find equal excitement in "Word-enriched praise." J. Oswald Sanders, in his excellent book *Prayer Power Unlimited,* explains, "The Scriptures are rich in material to feed and stimulate worship and adoration—especially the Psalms, which are God's inspired prayer books. As you read them, turn them into prayer. Vast tracts of truth await our exploration. Great themes abound—God's holiness, sovereignty, truth, wisdom, faithfulness, patience, love, mercy—all of which will call forth our worship."[10]

A Final Caution

As you begin to implement Scripture Praying be careful not to neglect other important aspects of prayer. Remember, our goal as prayer warriors is to develop a devotional habit that is complete and well-balanced. Some may find the excitement of Word-enriched prayer so fulfilling that little time is given for other serious prayer matters. Be careful not to neglect intercession, listening, praise, thanksgiving, and the other vital elements so essential to "complete" prayer. Yet, strive to give the Word of God its rightful place.

Lord, teach me to plead your promises!

Scripture Praying: The Fourth Step in World-Changing Prayer

1. When bringing Scripture into your devotional hour, ask God to bless His Word to your spiritual body, just as He blesses natural food to your physical body.
2. Examine a passage from either the Gospels, the Epistles, Psalms, or Proverbs. Look carefully for specific ways to apply each verse to prayer.
3. As you study a verse (or verses), ask yourself what petition this passage prompts you to make, or what promise this passage contains that stands directly behind a specific petition.
4. Develop actual prayers based on the thoughts and phrases included in a verse (or verses) of Scripture and offer those prayers confidently to the Lord.

6

Watching

The Act of Mental Awareness

Books on prayer seldom discuss, or even mention, the importance of "watching" in prayer. Yet Jesus commanded us to "watch and pray!" (Matt. 26:41; Mark 14:38).

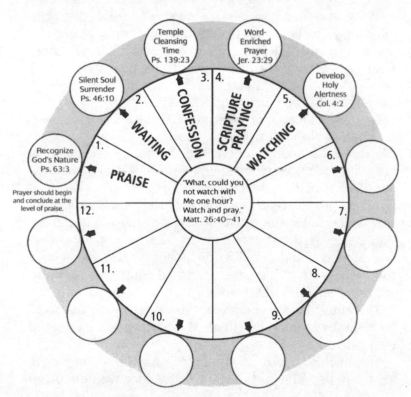

Temple Cleansing Time Ps. 139:23

Word-Enriched Prayer Jer. 23:29

Silent Soul Surrender Ps. 46:10

Develop Holy Alertness Col. 4:2

Recognize God's Nature Ps. 63:3

Prayer should begin and conclude at the level of praise.

3. 4.

2. CONFESSION

WAITING

SCRIPTURE PRAYING

5.

1. PRAISE

WATCHING

6.

12. "What, could you not watch with Me one hour? Watch and pray." Matt. 26:40–41 7.

11. 8.

10. 9.

Paul also challenged believers to "continue in prayer, and *watch in the same* with thanksgiving" (Col. 4:2, italics added). He made it clear that watching was to be a *specific* element of prayer, something as important to prayer as thanksgiving.

Be on the Alert

What did Jesus and His chief apostle mean when they challenged us to "watch" in prayer? The Greek word for our word *watch* is *gregoreo*, "to be awake or vigilant." The dictionary defines *watch* as "keeping awake in order to guard." It can also mean "a close observation" or "to be on the alert."

When Jesus and Paul used the expression *watch* they principally meant that believers should stay awake spiritually and keep guard. Since both Jesus and Paul linked watching with prayer, they were referring to staying alert during prayer. As one writer suggests, "Watching in prayer and supplication bespeaks having spiritual insight to discern the wiles of Satan and to discover the latter's end and means."[1]

When the apostle Peter warned us to be "vigilant" because Satan seeks to devour us (1 Peter 5:8), he used the very word *gregoreo* (translated "watch") which both Jesus and Paul used in conjunction with prayer.

After Paul spoke to the Ephesian Christians about putting on the full armor of God, he again stressed watching. Paul suggested they establish everything by "praying always with all prayer and supplication in the Spirit, and *watching thereunto* with all perseverance and supplication for all saints" (Eph. 6:18, italics added).

Dr. Curtis Mitchell explained, "To pray correctly one must be mentally alert and vigilant. Much praying is hampered by a dull, drowsy frame of mind."[2]

During this activity of watching our spiritual function is somewhat similar to the ministry of the "watchmen" in ancient Bible days. Concerning the city of Jerusalem God said, "I have set watchmen upon thy walls, O Jerusalem, which shall never hold their peace day nor night: ye that make mention of the LORD, keep not silence" (Isa. 62:6).

Appointing watchmen to guard walled cities was a common custom in Bible days. The watchman's chief responsibility was to warn the inhabitants of approaching enemies. The thought in Isaiah 62:6 is that God's prophets were like these watchmen. They could not hold their peace until the prophecy of God was fulfilled in the full restoration of Jerusalem. These watchmen stood alert to warn of impending spiritual conflict.

A Spirit of Watchfulness

Our first order of business during the watching phase of prayer is to make ourselves *aware* of the various ways Satan seeks to hinder the effectiveness of our prayer. From the earliest moments of prayer he comes on the attack, trying to draw our minds from the key issues of prayer. To watch in prayer is to become aware of these attacks and stand firmly against them.

We should especially guard against prayer that lacks purpose. Suddenly the many items on our prayer list seem empty or vague. Prayer becomes shallow. We find ourselves making statements about prayer, instead of claiming specific things in prayer.

Only as we develop a spirit of watchfulness can we recognize Satan's plan of attack and block his efforts. As a perceptive prayer warrior suggests, "Always be on the alert to travel toward the goal of prayer, to disallow any unwanted words from mixing in, and to keep yourselves from praying prayers that are not prayers at all."[3]

But watching in prayer goes beyond developing an alertness to the manner in which Satan may attack. From a practical standpoint, time should be allocated during prayer for a mental reflection concerning what is happening beyond our immediate world. Not only must we be *alert* to personal satanic attacks, but we must become *aware* of the "wiles of the devil" as they pertain to God's plan throughout the world.

Steps for Watching

There are two essential questions the prayer warrior should ask himself as he goes about the ministry of intercession. They are: "How much awareness do I have relative to the problems of world evangelism?" and, "Am I aware of how Satan is working to hinder God's workers?"

Because watching means "a close observation," we must develop a plan for prayer that helps us observe the needs around us much more specifically. Following are several suggestions that should help intercessors develop just such a plan.

First, endeavor to read material that makes you spiritually "aware" of specific world needs. Missionary journals and denominational reports can be of great assistance in developing this awareness. Every Home for Christ, the ministry I direct, engages several staff members around the world who do nothing but research specific needs of world evangelism. Such research is of enormous value in helping to inform concerned intercessors. A good deal of "prayer fuel" is available to help Christians pray intelligently.[4] The tragedy is that so much of it is neglected due to a lack of awareness or outright unconcern.

Second, during prayer strive to reflect mentally about "news" of the day. Daily newspapers, as well as radio, television news broadcasts, and the Internet contain certain items that have a definite bearing on God's work throughout the world. Economic problems, civil unrest, political changes, and even weather conditions can enter into the fulfillment of the Great Commission. Ask God to refresh your mind concerning current events that deserve special prayer attention.

Finally, and certainly *most* important, ask the Holy Spirit to show you exactly what you should claim in prayer and how you should claim it. None of the suggestions discussed in this book can be put fully to use apart from concentrated direction from the Holy Spirit. In fact, without the Holy Spirit guiding us, effectiveness in prayer is an impossibility.

Spiritual Prayer

Speaking on "spiritual prayer," Bishop J. C. Ryle expressed, "I commend to you the importance of praying spiritually. I mean by that, that we should labor always to have the help of the Spirit in our prayers, and be aware above all things of formality. There is nothing so spiritual but that it may become a form, and this is especially true of private prayer."[5]

There is nothing wrong with developing a consistent, systematic habit of prayer, as long as we carefully "watch" that our praying remains truly spiritual. Bishop Ryle adds, "If the skeleton and outline of our prayers be by habit, almost a form, let us strive that the clothing and filling up of our prayers be as far as possible of the Spirit."[6]

No discussion of the subject of watching in prayer can be complete without emphasizing the value of the Holy Spirit in prayer. Paul told Roman believers, "Likewise the Spirit also helpeth our infirmities: for we know not what we should pray for as we ought: but the Spirit itself maketh intercession for us with groanings which cannot be uttered. And he that searcheth the hearts knoweth what is the mind of the Spirit, because he maketh intercession for the saints according to the will of God" (Rom. 8:26–27).

It is clear from this passage that a prayer warrior is not left to himself in understanding the "how" of prayer. Each has been given the help of the Holy Spirit to guide and direct. This guidance is best cultivated in the watching aspect of prayer.

Twice in Scripture believers are admonished to "pray in the Spirit" (Eph. 6:18; Jude 20). Of course, praying in the Spirit, as I have discovered, means vastly different things to different Christians. The purpose here is not to evaluate this expression from a theological standpoint. Numerous books have exhausted this subject quite well. However, I do suggest the reader seek to develop a much enlarged recognition of the Holy Spirit's power as it relates to personal prayer.

No doubt the majority of Christians, no matter their theological persuasions, would agree with the statement of Lehman Strauss: "If anyone were to ask me what is the first truly great secret of a successful prayer life, I would say in answer, 'Praying in the Holy Spirit.'" The writer adds, "Human wisdom and human desire can achieve human results. But praying in the Spirit produces divine results."[7]

In reading biographies of past spiritual leaders it is obvious that praying in the Spirit was not treated lightly. Samuel Chadwick, a saint mightily used of God, spoke of a powerful encounter with the Holy Spirit in 1882. He called it "the key to all of my life." Of his experience Chadwick testified, "It awakened my mind as well as my heart. It gave me a new Bible and a new message. Above all else, it gave me a new understanding and a new intimacy in the communion and ministry of prayer; it taught me to pray in the Spirit."[8]

Let the reader especially note that Chadwick's spiritual encounter "awakened" his mind. The preacher immediately discovered truths about prayer he had never observed before. A new intimacy was experienced in daily prayer, something every believer should earnestly covet.

Perhaps the reason much of our praying becomes dull and lifeless is that we lack spiritual intimacy with the only Being who can add life to our praying. John Bunyan wrote, "It is the easiest thing in a hundred to fall from power to form, but it is the hardest thing of many to keep in the life, spirit and power of any one duty, especially prayer. It is such a work that a man *without the help of the Spirit* cannot do so much as pray once, much less continue without, in a sweet praying frame, and in praying, so to pray as to have his prayer ascend unto the ears of the Lord of the Sabbath."[9]

Seeing Things Invisible

God earnestly desires to reveal special secrets during prayer, to help us pray more specifically for particular needs. To "watch" in prayer is to open our spiritual eyes to perceive these secrets. We must permit the Holy Spirit to "enlighten" us during prayer. Professor Hallesby taught, "The spirit of prayer throws light upon every phase of our prayer life. Not only theoretical light, enlightening our minds, but practical light for our use in praying and for training in prayer."[10]

As we "watch" in prayer, those needs hiding in the shadows of human awareness come alive through the light of God's Spirit. We see each need with a supernatural clarity. What was once a blur is now in focus.

An entirely new dimension will soon be added to our praying. We will see what is not possible to see. Jonathan Swift said, "Vision is the art of seeing things invisible." Our praying suddenly has this unique, God-given "vision." Our imagination comes alive. By God's Spirit the mission field is not across the world, *we* are across the world—on that very mission field. We actually begin to feel the suffering being experienced by those for whom we pray.

Anne Townsend expressed this in her thought, "If I can imagine what it must be like to be the one for whom I am praying, then I find that I can begin to intercede for that person. My imagination leads me on to want to be more deeply involved with him in his own life. This involvement leads to caring, caring leads to love, and love leads to intercession."[11]

As we seek to "watch" in prayer God will enlarge the capacity of our imagination to see certain needs even more clearly. Scripture says, "But, as it is written, 'What no eye has seen, nor ear heard, nor the heart of man conceived, what God has prepared for those who love him,' God has revealed to us through the Spirit . . ." (1 Cor. 2:9–10 RSV).

Paul is reminding us that spiritual insight does not emerge from the inner resource of man's ability *unless* it is illuminated through the power of the Holy Spirit. This is why we must earnestly covet more of God's Spirit in our praying.

Inner Vision

As we develop the ministry of "watching" in prayer, whether we set aside two minutes or ten, soon God will call upon us to pray very special prayers. We should expect to see things that startle us.

Professor Hallesby shared an account that illustrates this thought. He spoke of an ordinary country girl, Bolette Hinderli, who had a most unusual prayer experience that ultimately brought thousands to Christ.

While in prayer the young girl experienced an inner vision of a man in a prison cell. She observed his face as plainly as the print on this page. Accompanying this vision was an inner voice that urgently declared, "This man will share the same fate as other criminals if no one takes up the work of praying for him. Pray for him, and I will send him out to proclaim my praises among the heathen."

Bolette Hinderli was obedient to the heavenly call. For months she prayed earnestly that the prisoner would learn of God. She carefully searched news articles and listened to testimonies of converted Christians. She hoped to hear of someone converted while in prison and now proclaiming the gospel.

Finally, during a trip to a distant city in Norway, Bolette Hinderli heard that a former prisoner, now converted to Christ, was scheduled to share the evening message in a local church. With quiet excitement Miss Hinderli sat in a pew, awaiting the message. Then, Lars Olsen Skrefsrud, the guest speaker for the evening, walked to the small pulpit. Bolette's heart exploded for joy. She immediately recognized the face of the man who preached. It was, without question, the very man for whom she had been praying.

We must depend daily on the Holy Spirit to enlarge our awareness in all matters of prayer. Let us follow the suggestion of Andrew Murray who challenged, "The great lesson for every time of prayer is—to see to it, first of all, that you commit yourself to the leading of the Holy Spirit, and with entire dependence on Him, give Him the first place; for through Him your prayer will have a value you cannot imagine, and through Him also you will learn to speak out your desires in the name of Christ."[12]

Lord, teach me to watch!

Watching: The Fifth Step in World-Changing Prayer

1. Take a few moments during prayer to become spiritually alert. Watch for the methods Satan may try to use to hinder your Christian walk that day. Prayerfully claim power to defeat Satan in each of these areas.
2. Read denominational or missionary-evangelism magazines to help become alert to specific needs in God's work around the world.

3. Prayerfully recall various international news developments that deserve special prayer.
4. Ask the Holy Spirit to reveal further spiritual facts about these needs. This will aid you in praying more intelligently for these needs.

7

Intercession

The Act of Earnest Appeal

A ndré Maurois, a French biographer, said, "The universe is indifferent. Who created it? Why are we here on this

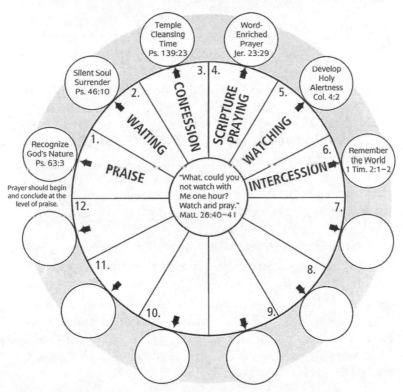

puny mud heap spinning in infinite space? I have not the slightest idea and I am quite convinced that no one has!"[1]

Fortunately, the follower of Christ knows his reason for being. We have both a divine task and a divine purpose. Our supreme "purpose" is to glorify God. Our supreme "task" is to evangelize the lost. In the truest sense, the latter most faithfully fulfills the former. To evangelize the lost glorifies God on the highest level.

This is why intercession (prayer for others) is so essential to the devotional habit. It might be labeled "the heart of prayer." Although intercession is only one aspect of prayer, because of its importance I have included a chapter on page 131 to help the reader further develop this essential aspect of prayer.

No Higher Plane

What is intercession? It is God's method for involving His followers more completely in the totality of His plan. In no other way can the believer become as fully involved with God's work, especially the work of world evangelism, as in intercessory prayer.

Basically, intercession is prayer offered on behalf of another. When the prayer warrior intercedes he forgets his personal needs and focuses all of his faith and prayer-attention on others.

To intercede is to mediate. It is to stand between a lost being and an almighty God, praying that this person will come to know about God and his salvation. As Edward Bauman explains in *Intercessory Prayer,* "When we pray for others we do not stand with outstretched hands hoping to receive something for ourselves. We stand at God's side, working together with Him, in the task of redeeming others."[2]

Surely there is no higher plane for prayer than intercession. What could be more important than participating in
the redemption of another being through prayer? True, our
prayer does not save the sinner, but somehow it serves to
prepare his heart for the moment word reaches him of
Christ's love. Search for a person who claims to have found
Christ apart from someone else's prayer, and your search
may go on forever.

The ministry of intercession, that of earnestly appealing
on behalf of another, is especially important because it is
the believer's common ground for Christian service. Spiritually speaking, prayer is the divine equalizer. Some preach,
others teach, a few sing publicly, but all can pray. Paul Billheimer reminds us, "Many people grieve because they have
been denied service on the mission field or in some other
chosen endeavor. But through faithful intercession they
may accomplish as much and reap as full a reward as
though they had been on the field in person."[3]

The Hallmark of Prayer

Intercession is the broadest scope of prayer. There is no
other mode of prayer that reaches out to *all* the world as
does intercessory prayer. E. M. Bounds explains, "Prayer
must be broad in its scope—it must plead for others. Intercession for others is the hallmark of all true prayer. . . . Prayer
is the soul of a man stirred to plead with God for men."[4]

In intercessory prayer we find the key to freedom for
those in bondage. Note the promise God gave Abimelech:
"He [Abraham] is a prophet, and he shall pray for thee, and
thou shalt live" (Gen. 20:7).

Could it be that our very prayers hold "life" for the unevangelized? Those directly involved in world evangelism would
answer a resounding yes. Ask almost any missionary if prayer
is important in his labor and be prepared to hear a sermon.

Dr. Yohann Lee, one-time president of Every Home for Christ, is a Korean Christian who was born in China where his family once served as missionaries. During his tenure Dr. Lee saw more than eight million written decisions result from home-to-home literature evangelism.

To what did Lee attribute these extraordinary results? Speaking specifically on the steadfastness of these many converts, Lee says, "The prayers of the saints directly affect the proportion and degree of the Holy Spirit's power over a newborn babe in Christ. *Prayer is where it all begins and where it all ends.*" A. T. Pierson adds, "Every step in the progress of missions is directly traceable to prayer. It has been the preparation for every new triumph and the secret of all success."

The Great Cry

But intercession is much more than merely praying for others. Interceding is engaging in actual battle.[5] There is a certain spirit of authority that must accompany a good deal of intercession. This thought is amplified by A. J. Gordon, "We have authority to take from the enemy everything he is holding back. The chief way of taking is by prayer, and by whatever action prayer leads us to. The cry that should be ringing out today is the great cry, 'Take, in Jesus' great Name!'"[6]

While visiting Communist China and walking the dusty paths of a rural commune, I was vividly reminded that Christ gave His life for those in the most remote places on earth. As I gazed across vast acres of Chinese farmland my heart recited, "The earth is the LORD's, and the fullness thereof" (Ps. 24:1).

I reminded myself that China really belongs to God. Satan has staged only a temporary invasion. Intercessors hold the power and authority to claim back what rightfully belongs to God, including all of China's 1.3 billion souls.

True, God could save China's masses in a moment, but He waits for praying saints to join Him in the battle. This is *His* plan, and those who believe God answers prayer must be at the heart of it.

But to be at the heart of God's plan for world evangelization requires much more than mere lip service. As intercessors we must go beyond the simple act of "praying for others" to the point of manifesting a genuine spirit of concern for others. Consider the example of Christ. Before our Lord ascended to heaven for the purpose of interceding on our behalf (Rom. 8:34), He first *gave* Himself to die on a lonely cross.

Thus, intercession begins with a spirit of giving before it becomes a spirit of praying. Francois Coillard explains, "Our prayers for the evangelization of the world are but a bitter irony so long as we give only of our superfluity, and draw back before the sacrifice of ourselves."[7]

Prayer Centered on Others

When Jesus taught His disciples to pray it was clear the emphasis was to be on others (Matt. 6:9–13). His prayer began with the plural possessive pronominal adjective— "our." We were not taught to pray, "*My* father," but, "*Our* Father!" Further in the prayer we see statements like "give *us*," "lead *us*," and "forgive *us*." In the deepest sense, the prayer is a love prayer. Every word is selfless. It cannot be prayed without deep compassion.

John Calvin declared, "Our prayer must not be self-centered. It must arise not only because we feel our own need as a burden which we must lay upon God, but also because we are bound up in love for our fellow men that we feel their need as acutely as our own. To make intercession for men is the most powerful and practical way in which we can express our love for them."[8]

To keep our praying always centered on others, intercession should come before petition. "We are all selfish by nature," explained J. C. Ryle, "and our selfishness is very apt to stick to us, even when we are converted. There is a tendency in us to think only of our own needs, our own spiritual conflicts, and our own progress in religion, and forget others."[9]

Because Jesus realized we would periodically lapse into a spirit of selfishness, he taught us to pray, "Thy kingdom come," before praying, "Give us this day our daily bread." Jesus wanted us to become "soul conscious" instead of "thing conscious." E. M. Bounds advises, "So also prayers for men are far more important than prayers for things because men more deeply concern God's will and the work of Jesus Christ than things."[10]

The Question of Repetition

When believers begin praying daily for unevangelized nations, it is not uncommon for their praying to sound strangely similar. After several weeks, or even just a few days, questions may arise concerning the matter of repetition in prayer. Is it wrong to repeat a prayer that is exactly the same as or similar to a prayer we have prayed previously? What did Jesus mean when He cautioned His followers concerning "vain repetition" in prayer?

Look carefully at the passage in question. Jesus said, "But when ye pray, use not vain repetitions, as the heathen do: for they think that they shall be heard for their much speaking" (Matt. 6:7).

It is not uncommon to hear some Bible teachers use this verse to suggest that all repetition in prayer is unscriptural. But look again at our Lord's exact words. Jesus did not actually condemn *all* repetition in prayer. Instead, He instructed His followers to avoid "vain" or "empty" repetition. He further qualifies the term *vain* by adding, "as the heathen do."

These four words reveal what kind of repetition is meaningless in prayer.

Various heathen cultures have strange and unique forms of prayer that are clearly empty and repetitious. The Tibetan Buddhist prayer wheel is most notable. Chiseling prayers to heathen gods on a clay wheel, and assuming that spinning the wheel causes these hundreds of prayers to rise simultaneously during each revolution, is a perfect example of "vain" repetition.

On the other hand, the Christian in right standing with Jesus, who brings before his Lord a similar petition from day to day, hardly finds himself in the same category as a wheel-spinning Buddhist. To pray similar prayers daily for various nations of the world cannot be classified as "vain" repetition. True, it may appear repetitious, but it is not vain.

The reader may be surprised to discover that repetition in prayer is even scriptural. In fact, Abraham failed in prayer because he gave up in his petitioning (Gen. 18:16–33). However, Elijah pleaded with God seven times and witnessed a remarkable outpouring from God (1 Kings 18:42–45). Commenting on these passages Jack Taylor asks, "Is it without significance that Elijah prayed seven times—the number of perfection and fullness—while Abraham stopped at six times, the number of human frailty?"[11]

Further, it is interesting to note that even our Lord repeated a prayer. In Gethsemane Christ offered a petition three times, "saying the same words" (Matt. 26:44). Twice Jesus prayed for a blind man (Mark 8:24–25). King David repeated a "prayer of praise" twenty-six times in Psalm 136.

Making Mention in Prayer

After spending numerous times in prayer with a former associate in our ministry, I was amazed to find that he prayed for every person on the Every Home for Christ headquarter's staff by name. He also prayed for each overseas leader associated with the ministry. Quietly and confidently he would appeal for compassion, wisdom, and strength for each of the scores of workers on his list. Wives of these workers were also included.

Then, with continuing confidence, he prayed for every major Christian leader who was even vaguely familiar to me. And there was more. He proceeded to intercede for every king, president, and political leader of the almost fifty Islamic and Communist nations at that time. He did not pray for the leaders collectively, but for each separately, *by name.*

Although the intensity and confidence of this praying blessed me, I realized some believers are troubled by the thought of lengthy prayer lists. They feel they are short-changing a need by simply "mentioning" the need briefly in prayer. Fortunately for my own prayer life, God directed my attention to a firm scriptural foundation for this very method of praying.

Not once, or twice, but four specific times the apostle Paul spoke of "making mention" of his fellow Christians in prayer. To Roman believers he wrote, "For God is my witness ... that *without ceasing* I make mention of you always in my prayers" (Rom. 1:9, italics added).[12]

Surely the apostle did not spend his entire waking time praying for every specific need of each fellow Christian. Instead, he confidently lifted their names before God, fully trusting God to bless each of them.

After observing the confident praying of this Christian brother, and discovering the scriptural basis for making mention in prayer, I was pleased to note that other prayer warriors have also witnessed great results through this type of praying. According to R. E. Speer in his book *Paul, the All-Round Man,* Bishop Handley Moule told of a dedicated Sunday school teacher who helped bring numerous students to a saving knowledge of Jesus. Following her death, the teacher's diary was found to contain, among other entries, these resolutions: "Resolved to pray for each scholar *by name*." "Resolved to wrestle in prayer for each scholar *by name*." "Resolved to wrestle for each *by name* and to expect an answer."[13]

Never be troubled by the fact that your knowledge of a need is somewhat limited. True, you should ask the Holy Spirit to aid you in prayer so that your praying is as meaningful and intelligent as possible. But don't become discouraged solely because your prayers lack the depth of understanding you desire. Above all, remember that all of prayer, especially intercession, is a learning experience. Professor Hallesby preached, "As far as my understanding of these things goes, intercessory prayer is the finest and most exacting kind of work that is possible for men to perform." This perceptive Bible teacher concluded, "Since intercessory prayer is such a fine and difficult art, it is not at all remarkable that it should require a long and rigorous period of training."[14]

Lord, teach me to intercede!

Intercession: The Sixth Step in World-Changing Prayer

1. Carefully prepare for intercession by developing a specific plan that includes special prayer for God's work around the world.
2. Summon a new compassion for these moments of intercession, so your praying will reach out to the lost with genuine concern.
3. Fill your intercession with the four key scriptural claims: Ask God to give more laborers to the harvest, to open doors for these workers, to bless them with fruit as the result of their efforts, and with finances to expand their work. (See page 131 for an explanation of these claims.)
4. Always endeavor to include specific countries and their leaders during your time of intercession.

8

Petition

The Act of Personal Supplication

"A sking is the symbol of our desire," related E. Stanley Jones. "Some things God will not give until we want them enough to ask."[1]

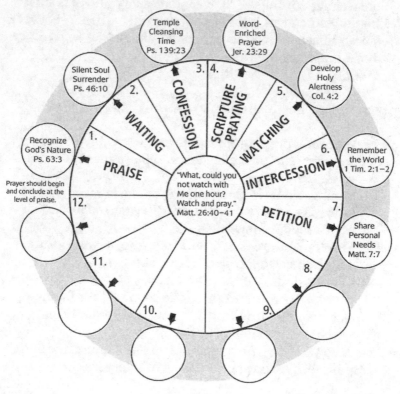

Petition is that aspect of prayer given over to asking God for specific personal things. To seek an unselfish spiritual or material blessing is not unscriptural. An obscure Old Testament passage illustrates. The passage is found amid a lengthy list of "begats." Commentaries declare that more than five hundred individual names are mentioned in the "begats" of 1 Chronicles. Yet, amid this somewhat exhaustive genealogy, God pauses to provide a brief look at one of these individuals, a man named Jabez.

The Bible says, "And Jabez was more honourable than his brethren: and his mother called his name Jabez, saying, Because I bare him with sorrow. And Jabez called on the God of Israel, saying, Oh that thou wouldest bless me indeed, and enlarge my coast . . . and that thou wouldest keep me from evil, that it may not grieve me! And God granted him that which he requested" (1 Chron. 4:9–10).

Nothing is mentioned about Jabez in Scripture other than that he sought a personal blessing of God and that it was granted. Such a testimony is not recorded of anyone else on this list of five hundred. Jabez was bold enough to entreat of God a blessing. God not only honored the request, but chose to use Jabez as an eternal example of how he longs to answer our sincere petitions.

The Rule of God

It is well said that "asking is the rule of the kingdom." The author of this phrase, Charles Spurgeon, adds, "It is a rule that will never be altered in anybody's case. If the royal and divine Son of God cannot be exempted from the rule of asking that He may have, you and I cannot expect to have the rule relaxed in our favor. God will bless Elijah and send rain on Israel, but Elijah must pray for it. If the chosen nation is to prosper, Samuel must plead for it. If the Jews are to be delivered, Daniel must intercede. God will bless Paul, and the nations shall be converted through him, but Paul must pray. Pray he did without ceasing; his epistles show that he expected nothing except by asking for it."[2]

In the same sense that our Christian experience is a "personal" experience, prayer, too, must become very personal. We must not hesitate to declare as Jabez, "Bless me, indeed!" When Jesus faced the blind man, He asked, "What wilt thou that I should do unto thee?" (Mark 10:51). Certainly our Lord knew the man's infirmity, but He wanted him to declare it.

This is petition. It is the confession of helplessness in a specific matter. As E. M. Bounds reminds us, "Prayer is the language of a man burdened with a sense of need. Not to pray is not only to declare that there is nothing needed, but to admit to a non-realization of that need."[3]

In a practical sense, petition is not the prayer of a man opening heaven's doors to release God's power. Rather, it is man opening his heart's door to receive power already appropriated by God. Expressed helplessness is the key to opening that door, thus giving God access to our need. *We must define the need.*

Expressed Dependence

Because petition is an expression of helplessness, it should be present each day in the devotional hour. Jesus taught us to pray, "Give us *this day* our *daily* bread" (Matt. 6:11, italics added).

E. M. Blaiklock explains that the Greek word for "daily" in Matthew 6:11 occurs almost nowhere else in any extant Greek text. According to Blaiklock, it appears only in a papyrus document, and there without a particular context. From its derivation the word seems to mean "of the morrow" or "of the coming day." The writer concludes, "The translation could well be: 'Give us today the bread of tomorrow.'"[4]

No matter what the full interpretation of Matthew 6:11 is, it is evident we are to express our dependence on Christ for every need. Personal petition is our means of such expression. During this aspect of prayer we are able to do as Job did when he "ordered" his cause before the Lord (Job 23:3–4). We go before God as an attorney with a carefully prepared argument upon which to base our case. We have a sincere, unselfish basis for our requests. Our motive is pure and our arguments well ordered. Spurgeon said, "The best prayers I have heard in our prayer meetings have been those which have been fullest of argument."[5]

Of course, to bring our arguments before God in prayer does not mean we are twisting God's arm in order to obtain a particular blessing. God desires that we present these "arguments" because we will learn the principles of prayer only by the actual practice of prayer. This may also be the reason God sometimes delays an answer to our prayers. He longs to answer our petitions, but He also desires to teach us much more about matters of true spiritual warfare. This prepares us for the really serious battles that lie ahead.

Keys to Petition

When offering personal petitions there are several principles that should be remembered.

First, *a petition should be specific.* Prayer must never be so vague that within minutes of our praying we have forgotten why we prayed. Andrew Murray suggests, "Let your prayer be so definite that you can say as you leave the prayer closet, 'I know what I have asked from the Father, and I expect an answer.'"[6]

To forget our purpose for praying is a sure indication of an absence of desire. The greater the intensity of our desire for a blessing, the greater the difficulty to blot the desire from our mind. If we can't remember what we asked for after we asked for it, perhaps we really didn't need it.

Next, *a petition should be complete.* Each request ought to be carefully thought through before it is presented. Avoid shallow petitions like, "Lord, bless me," or, "Lord, help the missionaries today." Instead, pray carefully through each request. It is spiritually healthy to take a need apart, piece by piece, during prayer. Analyze the problem from every angle and then express it as a petition. The more specific and complete the petition, the more faith is generated when we bring it to God.

Especially be careful that your petitions do not become sermons pointed heavenward. D. L. Moody said, "We hear a good deal of praying that is just exhorting God, and if you did not see the man's eyes closed, you would suppose that he was preaching. Much that is called prayer is not prayer at all. There needs to be more petition in our prayers."[7]

Third, *a petition should be sincere.* Personal attitudes are important in the matter of petition. It is true Jesus promises blessings to those who ask, seek, and knock, but we must strive to bring our claims before God with a right spirit. An unknown preacher expressed, "We are to ask with a beggar's humility, to seek with a servant's carefulness, and to knock with the confidence of a friend."

How sincere are we when we seek a specific blessing of God? Insincere praying is selfish praying. Andrew Murray cautioned, "One of the great reasons why prayer in the inner chamber does not bring more joy and blessing is that it is too selfish, and selfishness is the death of prayer."[8]

Finally, *a petition should be simple.* Although it was suggested earlier that we should analyze a problem, piece by piece, our manner of petition ought to be simple and informal. Long before an infant expresses its inner feelings in words, it cries out from within expressing needs in the simplest of terms. The offering of a petition should be complete enough to build faith, but simple in its expression. Eloquence is not necessary for effective praying.

A Child's Petition

Charles Spurgeon shared the account of a young lad who refused to doubt that God would answer even the simplest of petitions. At the start of the school term the local schoolmaster had repeatedly urged the children to be punctual. He promised to punish any child who was late.

Unfortunately, the parents of the boy made no effort to help the lad in these matters of discipline, and one day the child was considerably late for school. Just as his mother sent him through the door, the clock struck the very hour school was to begin.

A friend, standing nearby, saw the youngster running and heard his simple petition: "Dear God, do grant that I may be on time for school."

It occurred to the friend that for once the child had offered a prayer that was impossible for God to honor. Indeed, one cannot change the time. Still he was curious to see what might result.

Interestingly, it also happened that this very morning the schoolmaster, in trying to open the schoolhouse door, turned the key the wrong way and jammed the bolt. Unable to force it loose, he sent for the local locksmith. Precisely the moment the locksmith fixed the bolt, the lad arrived.

Even the simplest petition, when offered in faith, opens doors to the miraculous. God is greatly pleased when we come before His presence ready to ask of Him those petitions that will honor His name.

Lord, teach me to ask!

Petition: The Seventh Step in World-Changing Prayer

1. Begin your petitions by asking the Holy Spirit to help you claim only those desires that will bring special honor to the Lord.
2. Make a mental list of specific needs you have for that very day and offer each need to God.
3. Enlarge a petition carefully, taking time to explain to God why you desire an answer for that request.
4. Frequently examine your motives for claiming a petition. Be certain they are pure in the sight of God.

9

Thanksgiving

The Act of Expressed Appreciation

Although closely related to praise, thanksgiving itself is an important element that deserves careful attention during prayer. Basically, thanksgiving is the act of express-

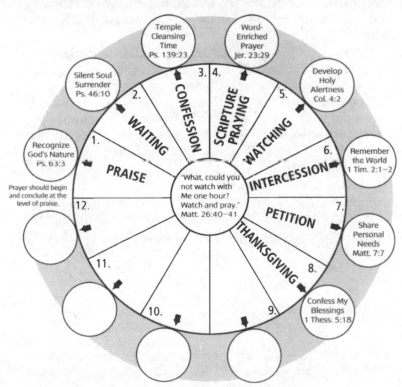

ing specific gratitude to God for blessings he has bestowed upon us. These expressions may be mental or vocal.

Thanksgiving differs from praise in that praise focuses on *who* God is, whereas thanksgiving focuses on *what* God has specifically done *for us*. As one writer explains, "When we give thanks we give God the glory for what He has done for us; and when we worship or give praise, we give God glory for what He is in Himself."[1]

The Attitude of Thanksgiving

The precise position for thanksgiving on our prayer schedule may vary. I have chosen to place it toward the end of my devotional hour as an expression of appreciation to God following my time of petition. Thanksgiving helps me focus on God's faithfulness.

However, a look at Scripture seems to suggest thanksgiving could be sprinkled throughout our praying. Paul told the Colossians, "As ye have therefore received Christ Jesus the Lord, so walk ye in him: Rooted and built up in him, and stablished in the faith, as ye have been taught, abounding therein with thanksgiving" (Col. 2:6–7). Later, he added, "Devote yourselves to prayer, keeping alert in it with an attitude of thanksgiving" (Col. 4:2 NASB).

Paul had a similar message for the church at Philippi. He instructed these believers: "Be careful for nothing; but in every thing by prayer and supplication with thanksgiving let your requests be made known unto God" (Phil. 4:6). According to Paul, all prayers should be filled with a "spirit of thanksgiving."

A Confession of Blessings

Thanksgiving might well be labeled "a confession of blessings." It is during this aspect of prayer that we recognize all of life's blessings and confess them before God. This is essential to prayer because it draws the heart to God, keeping it entirely centered on Him. Like praise, thanksgiving takes the believer's attention from self and places it where it must be centered to make prayer effective.

Thanksgiving is also important because it is the prayer warrior's special gift to God for His kindnesses. What else can we possibly give God other than praise and thanksgiving? The psalmist declared, "What shall I render unto the LORD for all his benefits toward me?" (Ps. 116:12). Later, he answers, "I will offer to thee the sacrifice of thanksgiving, and will call upon the name of the LORD" (Ps. 116:17).

In looking at the life of Christ it is evident that a spirit of thanksgiving was important to Him. In the Gospels we frequently see our Lord expressing gratitude. Describing the resurrection of Lazarus, the apostle John records, "Then they took away the stone from the place where the dead was laid. And Jesus lifted up his eyes, and said, Father, *I thank thee* that thou hast heard me" (John 11:41, italics added). Note Mark's description of Jesus feeding the multitude: "And he took the seven loaves, *and gave thanks*" (Mark 8:6, italics added).

On yet another occasion, after sharing important teaching with His disciples, Jesus paused to pray, "*I thank thee, O Father*, Lord of heaven and earth, because thou hast hid these things from the wise and the prudent, and hast revealed them unto babes" (Matt. 11:25, italics added). Surely that which was so important to our Savior should be considered essential to our devotional habit.

Thank Offerings

A wandering mind normally hinders effective praying, but if properly channeled it actually can prove helpful during your time of thanksgiving. Allow your mind to wander through the previous day's activities. This will lead you to many points of concentration for specific thanksgiving.

Also, become aware of all that exists around you. What do you see worthy of thanksgiving? In the same sense that we need to "watch" in prayer, or become alert to certain needs, we need to "watch" in thanksgiving. Become more aware of those specific things Jesus has done for you. Then verbalize these blessings.

Remember, thanksgiving begins when you mentally catalog the specific things God has done for you so you can put these blessings into words.

Following is a brief list of several "thank offerings" you might give God during your devotional hour:

First, *confess spiritual blessings.* What specific spiritual blessings has God given you recently? Perhaps He has bestowed a special blessing during this very devotional hour that is worthy of a word of appreciation. Take time during prayer to offer these blessings back to God in the form of vocal thanksgiving.

Second, *confess material blessings.* A moment should be given to consider the many material blessings God has generously provided. Be very specific, remembering even the little things. Thank Him for the chair in which you sit, or the warmth of the room. The more specific thanksgiving becomes, the more meaningful a role it will play in your devotional life.

Third, *confess physical blessings.* We should thank God specifically for good health. If we are free of pain or sickness, it is a blessing worthy of thanksgiving. If we are experiencing pain in one leg, we can express appreciation for strength in the other. We may thank God for good eyesight, or for the ability to hear. Each heartbeat or breath of air can be reason for thanksgiving. Like praise, thanksgiving is truly limitless.

Finally, *confess external blessings.* Some blessings are not directly related to us, but still they deserve an expression of appreciation. These might be termed external blessings. For example, thank God for kindnesses rendered to your friends, community, or nation. Above all, thank Him for His blessings on the work of evangelism around the world.

But especially strive to escape the tendency of generalized thanksgiving. Rather than declaring, "God, I thank you for blessing our church service last Sunday," magnify your thanksgiving. Let it include specific reasons why you are thankful.

Thanks for Past Blessings

An especially meaningful goal of thanksgiving is to thank God each day for at least one blessing you cannot remember thanking Him for previously. This will require a moment of quiet contemplation concerning God's goodness.

In seeking a point of focus for this type of thanksgiving, you may wish to look at past experiences. Perhaps God granted you specific favor or some particular blessing decades ago for which you never expressed thanks.

Do you recall ever thanking God specifically for the person who first told you about Jesus? Have you thanked God for your first Bible, or for the Sunday school teachers who encouraged you in your early years of faith?

Thanksgiving is further described as limitless by Paul's admonition to Ephesian believers, "Be filled with the Spirit . . . Giving thanks always for all things unto God" (Eph. 5:18, 20). To the Thessalonians Paul adds, "In every thing give thanks: for this is the will of God in Christ Jesus concerning you" (1 Thess. 5:18). John Wesley wrote in his journal that it was because of this attitude that he was able to thank God that he broke only his arm in an accident, and not his head.

In each situation of life, no matter the difficulty it presents, focus for thanksgiving can be discovered. Even the death of a loved one reminds us of the knowledge of eternal life, something for which we are truly thankful.

Let us carefully seek to develop this ministry of expressing appreciation to God during prayer. For every specific prayer of petition may we share two or three specific expressions of thanksgiving. God grant that we never cease to be grateful for His bountiful provisions.

Lord, teach me to give thanks.

Thanksgiving: The Eighth Step in World-Changing Prayer

1. Begin thanksgiving by thinking about all God has given you in recent days.
2. Use these moments of reflection as a basis for offering specific thanksgiving for spiritual, material, physical, and external blessings.
3. Frequently thank God "in advance" for blessings you expect Him to bestow on you in the future.
4. Thank God for at least one particular blessing you have not thanked Him for previously.

10

Singing

The Act of Melodic Worship

Words of adoration combined with a melody from the heart lead to praise in its most beautiful form. Martin Luther expressed it thus, "The gift of language combined

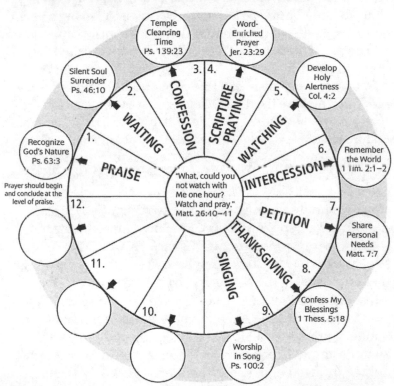

with the gift of song was given to man that he should proclaim the Word of God through music."

Here we discover one of the most neglected aspects of personal worship—singing alone in God's presence. The psalmist enjoined, "Serve the LORD with gladness: come before his presence with singing" (Ps. 100:2).

While many believers freely participate in congregational singing, few have discovered the joy of singing songs unto the Lord *during* prayer. The author was amazed to discover that only a few books on prayer from a collection exceeding 150 even mentioned singing, and then only in passing. Yet, no fewer than forty-one of the Psalms specifically refer to "singing praises" unto the Lord. In several of these Psalms the student of prayer can find three or four separate injunctions to "sing." Surely there must be power in giving a personal "song offering" to the Lord in private prayer.

The godly missionary Mary Slosser who worked with great diligence among the Chinese, spoke of the importance of music in her prayer life. She explained, "I sing the doxology and dismiss the devil!" Concerning the power of song, Amy Carmichael adds, "I believe truly that Satan cannot endure it and so slips out of the room—more or less!—when there is a true song. Prayer rises more easily, more spontaneously, after one has let those wings, words, and music, carry one out of oneself into that upper air."[1]

What should we sing during prayer? On two different occasions Paul spoke of "making melody" in our hearts unto the Lord with "spiritual songs" (Eph. 5:19; Col. 3:16). When Paul spoke of a spiritual song he was speaking of a song that originated in the believer's heart. The word *spiritual*, as used in these verses, means "inspired by the Spirit." Paul could not have been referring to the use of hymnbooks in public or private worship since hymnbooks were centuries away from publication when he wrote these words. Undoubtedly, hand-copied psalters were extremely scarce.

We recall also that Paul and Silas "sang praises" unto God while they were in prison (Acts 16:25). Surely there were no hymnbooks present in this damp cell. Their songs of praise were most certainly based on melodies created in their hearts. To these melodies were added personal words of praise.

The Weapon of Song

Singing unto the Lord during prayer is more than merely a fresh and exciting way to minister unto the Lord. It is actually a weapon of warfare that adds immense power to our praying. Note an Old Testament passage that supports this claim:

In 2 Chronicles 20 we read that Moab, Ammon, and the inhabitants of Mount Seir conspired to wage war on King Jehoshaphat of Judah. Upon hearing of the conspiracy, Jehoshaphat called the people of Judah to repentance. From across the nation they gathered for a time of prayer and fasting.

Through Jahaziel the prophet, God promised Jehoshaphat that Judah would see victory in battle. Full details of the battle are described in verses 20–22: "And they rose early in the morning, and went forth into the wilderness of Tekoa: and as they went forth, Jehoshaphat stood and said, Hear me, O Judah, and ye inhabitants of Jerusalem; Believe in the Lord your God, so shall ye be established; believe his prophets, so shall ye prosper. And when he had consulted with the people, he appointed singers unto the Lord, and that should praise the beauty of holiness, as they went out before the army, and to say, Praise the Lord; for his mercy endureth for ever. And *when they began to sing and to praise*, the Lord set ambushments against the children of Ammon, Moab, and Mount Seir, which were come against Judah; and they were smitten" (italics added).

Later, the narrative relates that Judah's troops arrived at the front lines of battle only to discover the enemy was already defeated. God may have sent angelic hosts to fight the battle since there is no evidence of other troops helping Judah win the campaign.

Key to this account are the words of verse 22, "And when they began to sing and to praise, the LORD set ambushments. ..." The victory *began* and *ended* with musical worship. So great was the blessing of victory that Scripture declares, "And when Jehoshaphat and his people came to take away the spoil of them, they found among them in abundance both riches... and precious jewels... *more than they could carry away*" (2 Chron. 20:25, italics added).

When the campaign was fully concluded Jehoshaphat and the people of Judah named the valley *Berachah*, which means "blessing." Indeed, the ministry of song when properly used in the devotional habit is a weapon that always leads to blessing.

Themes for Song

How do we make singing unto the Lord practical in the daily devotional habit? Of course, the singing of well-known hymns or popular choruses, from memory or with the aid of a hymnbook or chorus sheet, is a possibility. However, this may tend to add unwanted form to this aspect of prayer, in the same sense that reading someone else's prayers often drains life from our praying.

Rather, ask the Holy Spirit to create "new" melodies within your heart. With these melodies you will be able to sing songs based on a variety of themes.

The Bible lists at least six distinct themes that might be used in ministering unto the Lord with song. You need not sing songs based on all of these themes during every prayer time, although the list does reveal the vast scriptural foundation for such worship.

Songs of Praise

First, *sing praises unto the Lord*. Such was the worship of Paul and Silas in jail (Acts 16). The psalmist declared, "Praise the LORD; for the LORD is good: *sing praises unto his name;* for it is pleasant" (Ps. 135:3, italics added). During this singing phase of prayer, you may wish to *sing* praises to God instead of speaking them. As suggested, allow the melody to flow from your heart. Do not be concerned if your voice seems somewhat unpleasant.

On a number of occasions when my daughters were younger, they would sing songs to their father. Often these songs were actually composed *while* they were being sung. Equally often, the presentation was slightly off key. Yet, I was always delighted when they came to me with their special songs. Each song was special because of the sincerity of heart behind it, and because the singers were objects of their father's affection.

So it is with our "spiritual" singing. To sing praises unto the Lord brings great joy to God's heart because of His intense love for us.

Songs of Power and Mercy

Second, *sing of God's power and mercy*. "But I will sing of thy power," declared the psalmist. "Yea, I will sing aloud of thy mercy in the morning: for thou hast been my defense and refuge in the day of my trouble" (Ps. 59:16). Note the psalmist not only speaks of singing, but of singing *aloud*. The thought is that our song is not to be confined only to the heart. It is to be a vocal praising of God with melody.

To sing of God's *power* is to put into song all that God has accomplished with His power. To sing of His *mercy* is to sing of His faithfulness and justice. It is to sing the attributes of His divine nature. Indeed, all that God is can become a theme for a personal "spiritual" song.

Songs of Thanksgiving

Third, *sing a song of thanksgiving.* Look again at the words of the psalmist: "Sing unto the LORD *with thanksgiving;* sing praise upon the harp unto our God" (Ps. 147:7, italics added). As suggested in earlier chapters, praise is to recognize God for who He is. Thanksgiving, on the other hand, is to recognize God for what He has done for us. In singing "with thanksgiving" we create a song based on those specific gifts or blessings God has provided.

Sadly, few believers have ever experienced the joy of thanking God in song for little things like food and clothing. Anything we can thank God for verbally, we can thank God for musically.

Do not hesitate to combine the aspects of thanksgiving and singing periodically during your devotional hour. Sing specific "thank-yous" to the Lord for His generous gifts.

Songs of God's Name

Fourth, *sing the name of God.* To sing the name of the Lord in a song is scriptural. The psalmist testified, "I will praise the name of God with a song, and will magnify him with thanksgiving" (Ps. 69:30).

As suggested in our earlier discussion of praise, the "name" of the Lord in the Old Testament may be a direct reference to the name God took upon Himself when coming to earth in the form of His Son. The Bible says, "God was in Christ" when He reconciled the world (2 Cor. 5:19).

This makes it possible to praise the name of the Lord Jesus Christ in song. All that Jesus is or did can become the theme of our singing during our time alone in God's presence.

Songs of God's Word

Fifth, *sing God's Word.* The psalmist speaks once again of the power of song: "Thy statutes have been my songs in the house of my pilgrimage" (Ps. 119:54). To put melody to God's Word is another excellent way to worship God in song. We know that Christians of the early church were admonished to sing Scripture. James advised, "Is any among you afflicted? let him pray. Is any merry? let him sing psalms" (James 5:13). Surely this admonition does not apply only to singing in a gathering of believers. A person can be afflicted alone as well as with the congregation. If he is alone and afflicted, he is to pray. Similarly, if *any* (note the emphasis on the singular) *is merry, let him sing.* Any believer who is happy in Christ has at least one theme for a personal song during prayer. He can express his joy in a spiritual song.

Songs of My Heart

Finally, *sing a new song.* The psalmist shared, "I will sing a new song unto thee, O God: upon a psaltery and an instrument of ten strings will I sing praises unto thee" (Ps. 144:9).

"New" refers to something fresh. "A new song" means "my own song," not someone else's. It refers to a song from my heart that I have never sung before. Yesterday's song does not qualify under this category of singing. The theme may be similar but the song will be new. Of course, all the various themes for singing may fall under this category if we have never sung the melody or words previously. Even the singing of a scripture in a new way can be a "new song" from my heart.

Sing Among the Nations

Only the imagination can limit our singing "new songs" unto the Lord. A friend shared with me how God led her to use a map of the world during her time of singing. For more than two hours she sang through a listing of the more than two hundred countries on the map. Her song was simple. She sang of God's glory flowing into each nation. The melody was created "new" in her heart.[2]

She explained this was one of the most beautiful times of worship that she remembers. The song was one she had never sung before. Perhaps, by the Holy Spirit, she was fulfilling the expression of the psalmist, "I will sing unto thee among the nations" (Ps. 57:9). Through singing her special song this friend experienced a new joy in her devotional life.

Indeed, singing unto the Lord is especially important because it trains us in many new areas of worship. Ultimately, worship will be our *eternal purpose* in heaven, and singing will be a great part of this eternal purpose. In fact, note the description Isaiah gives of believers entering Zion, "Therefore the redeemed of the Lord shall return, and come with singing unto Zion; and everlasting joy shall be upon their head: they shall obtain gladness and joy; and sorrow and mourning shall flee away" (Isa. 51:11).

If singing is to play so vital a role in heaven's worship, surely it would do the believer well to "practice up" for the day we unite together in heavenly song to minister unto the Lord in our eternal Zion.

Lord, teach me to sing!

Singing: The Ninth Step in World-Changing Prayer

1. Pause in your devotional hour to sing a specific song unto the Lord.
2. Select a special theme for your song, such as praise, thanksgiving, or a favorite passage of Scripture.
3. Ask the Holy Spirit to create an original melody in your heart so your song is truly "a new song."
4. Don't hesitate to sing "songs of thanksgiving" for specific blessings or victories you believe God will give you in the days ahead.

11

Meditation

The Act of Spiritual Evaluation

The devotional hour is greatly strengthened when the believer takes time to ponder a spiritual theme in reference to God. This act of spiritual evaluation, called

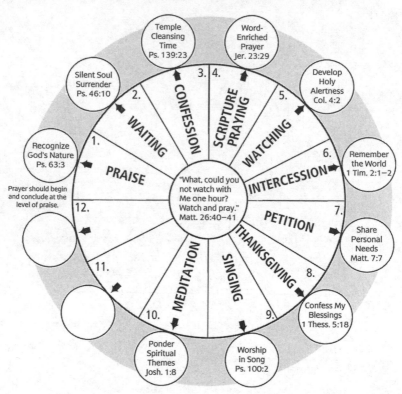

meditation, helps the believer discover how to apply all the truths God has revealed during prayer.

A century ago the wife of a Presbyterian minister, Bridgid E. Herman, wrote this meaningful description of meditation, "Meditation is a spiritual act as definite and purposeful as a business engagement, a pledge of friendship, or a solemn undertaking. In it we apply spiritual facts and principles to ourselves as individuals and as citizens of the Kingdom of God. Having pondered them, we seek to appropriate their value by an outgoing of our loving desires toward God, and by exercising our will in the formation of resolutions. No meditation is really valid unless it leaves us with something to which we can return during the day's business and find it helpful there."[1]

The Gift of Attention

While studying scores of books on prayer I was greatly disappointed to discover that almost as little is said about meditation as singing, although both aspects are thoroughly scriptural.

The Old Testament definition for the word *meditation* is "to mutter" or "to muse." This suggests a silent inner study of some spiritual matter. This is the essence of the meaning of "meditate" in Joshua 1:8: "This book of the law shall not depart out of thy mouth; but thou shalt meditate therein day and night, that thou mayest observe to do according to all that is written therein: for then thou shalt make thy way prosperous, and then thou shalt have good success." Here, the Hebrew word for "meditate" *(hagah)* means "to mutter upon."

Another Hebrew expression translated "meditate" is *sicah*, which means "to bow down." The psalmist used this word when declaring, "I will meditate in thy precepts, and have respect unto thy ways" (Ps. 119:15). The thought is that we render special "mental attention" by bowing down in respect of God's Word.

In the New Testament *meditation* is emphasized in Paul's admonition to Timothy, "Meditate upon these things; give thyself wholly to them; that thy profiting may appear to all" (1 Tim. 4:15). In this verse the Greek word for "meditate," *meletao*, means "to be careful," or "to show care" in a matter. This suggests meditation is more than merely thinking good thoughts. It is the giving of attention to how we might specifically apply these ponderings after the devotional hour has ended.

The Value of Meditation

Scriptural meditation provides the believer with spiritual benefits received through no other means. Personal inner peace is but one of these benefits. The Bible promises, "Thou wilt keep him in perfect peace, whose mind is stayed on thee" (Isa. 26:3). Enlarging on this verse, E. M. Blaiklock explains, "Here the Hebrew is actually saying, 'peace, peace,' thus making up for its deficiency in adjectives by the repetition of the noun. It might well have been translated literally—'in peace, in peace, I repeat . . .'"[2]

Throughout Scripture frequent attention is given to this matter of meditation: "How precious also are thy thoughts unto me, O God! how great is the sum of them! If I should count them, they are more in number than the sand: when I awake, I am still with thee" (Ps. 139:17–18).

Earlier the psalmist declared, "My meditation of him shall be sweet: I will be glad in the LORD" (Ps. 104:34). He also declared, "In the multitude of my thoughts within me thy comforts delight my soul" (Ps. 94:19).

The person who spends time thinking thoughts of God will find tremendous depth and understanding that will touch all areas of his life. It is, after all, in meditation that we rise above ourselves (and the world) for the purpose of seeing God's plan in proper perspective. Only from such a vantage point can we see the spiritual realm clearly. Bridgid E. Herman reminds us, "Self-regard is the slum of the soul, and the supreme function of meditation is to lift us out of its squalor into the clear, pure air of the spiritual world."[3]

Meditation is equally meaningful because it allows the believer to cultivate a harvest of fresh creative thoughts. As Oliver Wendell Holmes explained, "A man's mind stretched with a new idea can never go back to its original dimensions."

The Interior of Prayer

"To think well," Thomas Traherne said, "is to serve God in the interior court." Meditating with a solidly biblical foundation is the best thinking in which man can engage.

Bridgid Herman further explains, "The difference between the saints of old and ourselves is not one of inherent nature: it is simply that they took time to ponder God, to gaze upon Him in an act of supreme attention in which intelligent will and desire concurred in perfect harmony, while we are too greatly overrun with small activities and occupations to find leisure for such pondering."[4]

The author also advises, "To come to our own case. Behind all true Christian service—service, that is, springing from a sense of Divine vocation and sustained by a supernatural motive—lies the interior life of prayer. And if that prayer life, and therefore the service that springs from it, is feeble and ineffective, it is largely because it lacks the background of genuine honest thinking."[5]

Scripture provides the believer with a meaningful list of practical themes upon which to focus our meditation. Like other suggestions shared in these chapters, it is not necessary to implement all of these types of meditation during every devotional hour. However, the list is practical because it is scriptural. For a well-balanced devotional hour select at least one aspect each day as a focus for your meditation.

Focus on God Himself

First, *focus meditation on God Himself.* Speaking of meditation the psalmist declared, "My soul, wait thou only upon God; for my expectation is from him" (Ps. 62:5).

Earlier it was suggested that the believer take time to *wait* in prayer for the purpose of focusing love entirely upon God. Now, we return in prayer to enlarge that focus. At first glance it may appear that waiting and meditation overlap in their functions. However, *waiting* is an act of loving, while *meditation* is an act of thinking.

During this particular type of meditation ponder the nature of God with full intensity. Carefully probe everything you know about your heavenly Father, constantly asking the Holy Spirit to illuminate and stretch your thinking.

In the course of this type of meditation you will often find yourself asking many questions. What do I really believe about God? What does the Bible say about God that touches my life? How would I define my concept of God? What great attributes of God can I better appropriate in my daily life? As you answer these and other questions about God, your understanding of His nature and purpose increases dramatically, as does your confidence in His Word.

Focus on God's Word

Second, *focus meditation on God's Word.* The first two verses of the Psalms lead us to this focus of meditation: "Blessed is the man that walketh not in the counsel of the ungodly, nor standeth in the way of sinners, nor sitteth in the seat of the scornful. But his delight is in the law of the LORD; and in his law doth he meditate day and night" (Ps. 1:1–2).

Because meditation is the mental evaluation of any spiritual theme, the Bible becomes a tremendous source for meditation. Scripture is filled with thousands of brief phrases that inspire enormous power. Altogether, nearly thirty thousand promises await us in Scripture. Each promise is a focus for meditation. F. W. Faber expressed that one commonplace truth, seemingly tame and trivial to the beginner of meditation, will suffice a saint for hours of contemplation.

Speaking of the power of God's Word in meditation, Bridgid Herman enlarges, "The Book has a voice of its own— a message and a power that remain untouched by the passage of time. To listen to that voice and test that power for oneself is well worth all the labor and discipline involved."[6]

Focus on God's Works

Third, *focus meditation on the works of God.* The psalmist expressed, "I will meditate also of all thy work, and talk of thy doings" (Ps. 77:12). Here is another form of meditation that proves limitless. Every created aspect of the universe can become a focal point for effective meditation. But always, these ponderings must be in reference to God. We do not meditate on the beauty of a mountain stream simply because of the stream's beauty, but because of the stream's Creator.

An experience from the life of the sixteenth-century monk Brother Lawrence illustrates. "He told me," said an intimate friend, "that in the winter, seeing a tree stripped of its leaves, and considering that within a little time the leaves would be renewed and after that the flowers and fruit appear, he received a high view of the Providence and power of God which has never since been effaced from his soul. This view had set him perfectly loose from the world, and kindled in him such a love for God that he could not tell whether it had increased in above forty years that he had lived since."[7]

Focus on Past Victories

Fourth, *focus meditation on past victories*. Here is a seldom-mentioned aspect of meditation that will provide an oasis of delight for your devotional hour. The psalmist shared succinctly, "I remember the days of old" (Ps. 143:5).

In times of distress and discouragement much spiritual relief can be found in looking at the many blessings God has given us in previous days.

Consider Jeremiah's difficult experiences as recorded in Lamentations. Indeed, the very word *lamentation* means brokenness, pain, or grief. Of the five painful chapters in the book, perhaps the most distressing is chapter 3. Here the prophet speaks of God pulling him in pieces and of all his bones being broken. A particularly graphic verse reads, "He hath also broken my teeth with gravel stones, he hath covered me with ashes" (Lam. 3:16).

But notice the pause in the narrative that transforms Jeremiah's desert experience into a garden of blessings. In the midst of his complaints the prophet declares, "*This I recall to my mind*, therefore have I hope. It is of the LORD's mercies that we are not consumed, because his compassions fail not. They are new every morning; great is thy faithfulness" (Lam. 3:21–23, italics added).

Jeremiah discovered the secret of retrospective meditation. "This I recall," the prophet wrote during his battle with depression. When he had reached the point of total defeat he reflected on the past faithfulness of God. Because of this, Jeremiah was able to testify, "Great is thy faithfulness!"

We can do little during prayer that will add more beauty and freshness to our daily experience than will a moment sanctified to ponder past victories in Jesus. Sometimes a former experience will come alive with such reality that we almost relive the experience. The end result is a new confidence to face even the most difficult future.

Focus on Positive Thoughts

Finally, *focus meditation on positive thoughts*. Paul told his Philippian friends, "Finally, brethren, whatsoever things are true, whatsoever things are honest, whatsoever things are just, whatsoever things are pure, whatsoever things are lovely, whatsoever things are of good report; if there be any virtue, and if there be any praise, think on these things" (Phil. 4:8).

Anything worthy of praise is worthy of meditation. For example, some are lovers of little children. They may see the glory of God in a baby's eyes. Let them begin their time of meditation by setting a small child—perhaps the child they love best—in the midst of their many thoughts.

Any thought that meets the measure of Philippians 4:8 may serve as a focus for meditation. Teaching received in a Sunday school class or excerpts from a Christian periodical make excellent "food for meditation." Even a distraction during prayer may serve as fuel to ignite the flames of meaningful meditation.

If, during your time of spiritual evaluation, a distressing thought repeatedly buffets the mind, make that thought a special point for meditation. With God's help, walk through the problem step by step until a solution is discovered. Soon, meditation will become a practical way to visualize new avenues for sound spiritual growth.

Lord, teach me to meditate!

Meditation: The Tenth Step in World-Changing Prayer

1. Select a theme for your time of meditation, applying full attention to that specific area of spiritual thought.
2. Allow your mind to wander within the framework of your chosen theme. Ponder all aspects of the theme carefully in reference to God.
3. Ask questions about this theme that might lead you into an even deeper mental study of the subject.
4. Bring Scripture into all phases of meditation. This strengthens your awareness that God's Word is the necessary foundation for all meaningful spiritual thought.

12

Listening

The Act of Mental Absorption

"Prayer is the soul's pilgrimage from self to God; and the most effectual remedy for self-love and self-absorption is the habit of humble listening."[1] These words, written

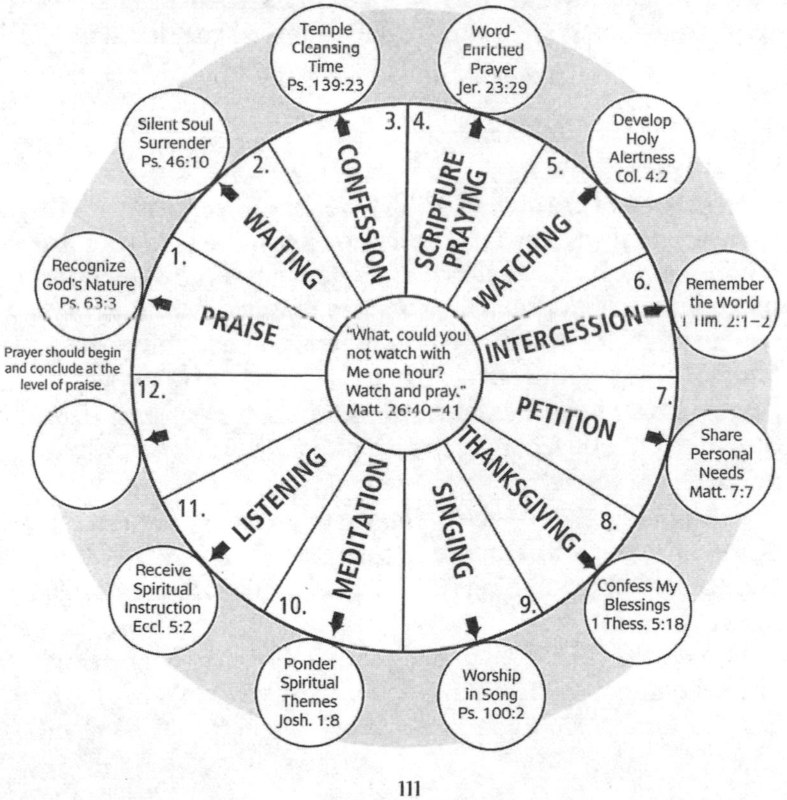

Temple Cleansing Time Ps. 139:23
Word-Enriched Prayer Jer. 23:29
Silent Soul Surrender Ps. 46:10
Develop Holy Alertness Col. 4:2
Recognize God's Nature Ps. 63:3
Remember the World 1 Tim. 2:1–2
Prayer should begin and conclude at the level of praise.
Share Personal Needs Matt. 7:7
Receive Spiritual Instruction Eccl. 5:2
Confess My Blessings 1 Thess. 5:18
Ponder Spiritual Themes Josh. 1:8
Worship in Song Ps. 100:2
1. PRAISE
2. WAITING
3. CONFESSION
4. SCRIPTURE PRAYING
5. WATCHING
6. INTERCESSION
7. PETITION
8. THANKSGIVING
9. SINGING
10. MEDITATION
11. LISTENING
12.
"What, could you not watch with Me one hour? Watch and pray." Matt. 26:40–41

over a century ago, bring us to that element of prayer called *listening*. Many centuries earlier, Solomon penned, "Be not rash with thy mouth, and let not thine heart be hasty to utter any thing before God: for God is in heaven, and thou upon earth: therefore let thy words be few" (Eccles. 5:2).

In our study of the devotional hour it becomes evident that certain elements of prayer seem quite similar. Some might wonder how listening differs from either waiting or meditation.

As stated, waiting is to thoughtfully focus attention on God in a love relationship. It is a time of resting silently in God's love. On the other hand, meditation is a very careful exploration of a particular spiritual theme. Though closely related to both, listening is an element of prayer that stands alone. To listen in prayer is to mentally absorb divine instructions from God concerning specific matters for that day.

The University of Silence

Best friends are always good listeners. If we truly desire to be friends with the Lord, we must learn the secret of listening. Not only did Jesus say He would enter the open door of a person's heart, but He promised to "sup" with that person as well (Rev. 3:20). To sup means to have fellowship. Much of our praying consists of *asking* instead of *supping*. Prayer often becomes one-sided and self-centered. Our prayer should be a conversation, one in which we listen as much as we speak.

Rosalind Rinker advises, "Instead of each of us making a prayer speech to Him, let's talk things over with Him, back and forth, including Him in it, as we do when we have a conversation."[2]

In a certain sense, listening is an actual ministry. Jesus ministered through listening. As Hope MacDonald explains in *Discovering How to Pray*, "Jesus listened to the cry of the blind man in the crowded noisy street. He listened to the story of Mary Magdalene when she came uninvited to a dinner party. He listened to the plea of the lepers when no one else would go near them. Jesus also listened to Nicodemus, who came to talk to Him late one night. Our Lord even listened to the thief hanging next to Him when He was dying on the cross."[3]

To be like Jesus is to be a listener, especially in prayer. The desire of Jesus was to do the will of His Father. To find His Father's will Jesus spent whole nights listening.

We, too, must follow the example of Jesus and learn the art of listening in God's University of Silence. Paul told the Thessalonians, ". . . study to be quiet" (1 Thess. 4:11). J. R. Miller explains, "Quietness in a man or a woman is a mark of strength. Noise is not eloquence. Loudness is not power. In all the departments of life, it is the quiet forces that effect most. Therefore, if we would be strong, we must learn to be quiet. A quiet heart will give a quiet life."[4]

The Gift of Listening

To quiet our hearts for the specific purpose of receiving the day's guidance is an act of both dependence and faith. Listening implies confidence that God truly desires to speak to us. It also serves to move our devotional habit still further from an emphasis on self. Alan Redpath confesses, "Sometimes I wonder if our devotions are not the greatest barrier to spiritual growth, because they are so often just one-sided—it is our praying, it is our talking, our Bible study, our effort. How long is it since you sat down with great delight in His presence and were conscious that He was flooding your heart and speaking with you?"[5]

Only as we learn to hear the voice of the Father can we learn to dispel the voices of the world. As David Hubbard shares, "We are besieged by words in our society. Billboards blaze them into our minds as we go by. Headlines scream from the newspapers. The internet is an avalanche of words. Regular prayer builds into our lives those experiences of silence and concentration when the still, small voice of our Saviour can cut through life's howl and speak His words of peace and joy."[6]

Of necessity, much of prayer must take place in silence because much of prayer concerns the believer seeking divine guidance. Not only will God reveal how to pray effectively, if we will listen, but He will reveal how to *live* effectively.

Donald E. Demaray refers to this listening aspect of prayer as the law of the inner voice. He explains, "Individual guidance from God, received in prayer, is of vital importance. And how easy it is to listen to your own voice pressing you to do the selfish things! But it is the voice of God—the inner voice—we must learn to hear. The regular quiet time is the laboratory for developing that capacity to 'hear.' In the course of the busy day, too, we will hear His voice, but it is in the stillness of the prayer closet that the gift of listening is given and received."[7]

God, alone, knows the solution to every problem we will face. This listening phase of prayer allows the believer to tune in on God's solutions. Carefully guard your devotional hour from becoming a soliloquy of selfishness. We do not engage in prayer to tell God what to do. Our goal in prayer is to discover what God wants us to do so that He will be glorified.

The Price of Silence

God mightily used Moses because he was "very meek." More than this, as Scripture relates, Moses was meek "above all the men which were upon the face of the earth" (Num. 12:3). Here was an old man, eighty years of age, and yet God chose Moses to lead an army of several million. Why? Because Moses was "meek," and the meek person is a listener.

John Anthony Hanne adds this insight: "There were men like Aaron who were eloquent preachers, men like Korah who were natural leaders, but only one man that recognized that he couldn't lead unless God first spoke to him and then spoke through him. Day after day for 40 years, dwelling upon what God had said, Moses listened and so spoke. Small wonder that through Moses came more of the Bible than any other man."[8]

Awesome power awaits the Christian who develops a listener's spirit. But because this spirit leads to such power the price to obtain it is high. Describing this spirit Peter relates, "A meek and quiet spirit . . . is in the sight of God of great price" (1 Peter 3:4).

What is the price of silence, but the gift of self to God? It is to shut our eyes to what the world considers important and listen only to the Holy Spirit's call.

The price of silence is also time, much time given to the practice of listening. A praying saint wrote, "Prayer of positive, creative quality needs a background of silence, and until we are prepared to practice this silence, we need not hope to know the power of prayer."[9]

In an active world nothing seems more difficult than "soul listening." The closer we come to the conclusion of our devotional hour the more our minds cry out for action. Let us listen carefully to be certain all of our plans for action originate in God.

The Whisperings of God

Since the sounds of the world wreak havoc in our prayer, the secret of silence begins in conquering these undesirable sounds. F. W. Faber declares, "Whenever the sounds of the world die out in the soul, then we hear the whisperings of

God. He is always whispering to us, only we don't always hear because of the noise, hurry and distractions which life causes as it rushes on."[10]

How will God speak during these times of stillness? Often His whisperings come in the form of a quiet impression on the heart. Elijah heard God speak with the "sound of a gentle whisper" (1 Kings 19:12 LB). But His whispering was very specific, as God gave Elijah guidance for that particular moment in his experience.

On other occasions there is no inner voice to guide us, yet we sense God's presence gently leading. We know that to move in a certain direction will please God, and so we follow this quiet leading.

Most often God speaks through His Word. In fact, all forms of guidance must be measured by Scripture. Guidance contrary to God's Word is guidance originating from another source.

A Practical Function

During the listening aspect of prayer you may wish to keep a note tablet handy to record these impressions concerning your day. If a housewife asks God to help her plan the day's activities, she should be ready to jot down any divine promptings. The businessman who questions which important project demands the most careful attention for the day should ask God to give him specific wisdom for that specific day's responsibilities.

Always remember, listening serves a practical function. You are not merely listening for divine "niceties," but you are asking God to order your day. The value of having paper and pencil is that it displays faith. It says to God, "I believe you will truly speak to me, and I have come prepared to record your instructions."

True, there are dangers to be faced when we enter these deeper aspects of prayer. Much of prayer is an experiment in spiritual growth that involves both failure and success. But if we persevere, the blessings will transcend all disappointments. Our knowledge of God will increase and abound beyond measure. As Bridgid Herman so accurately states, "One hour of such listening may give us a deeper insight into the mysteries of human nature, and a surer instinct for Divine values, than a year's hard study or external intercourse with men."[11]

Lord, teach me to listen!

Listening: The Eleventh Step in World-Changing Prayer

1. In the "listening" time of prayer do not hesitate to ask God very specific questions about difficult problems or situations.
2. Search Scripture for specific answers to your questions. God most often speaks through His Word.
3. Mentally evaluate all circumstances that relate to a problem. Ask God to show you His plan through those circumstances.
4. Be prepared to write down any ideas God may share concerning the details of solving that particular problem.

Praise

The Act of Divine Magnification

Prayer has now come full circle, and we find ourselves again at praise. Worship should seal all praying. We

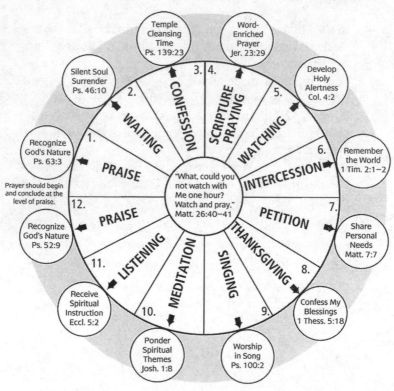

began with an act of adoration, and we will end with an act of magnification.

When Mary received word she would give birth to the Son of God, divine worship exploded from her lips: "My soul doth magnify the Lord, and my spirit hath rejoiced in God my Saviour. . . . For he that is mighty hath done to me great things; and holy is his name" (Luke 1:46–49).

Jesus not only taught us to begin our prayer with praise— "Our Father which art in heaven, Hallowed be thy name," but He also taught us to end our praying with praise—"For thine is the kingdom, and the power, and the glory, for ever. Amen" (Matt. 6:9, 13).

Prayer's Final Moments

As we come to these final moments of prayer, the soul pauses to contemplate the awesome wonder of God's being. We vocally magnify the nature of God. To magnify the Lord's name with praise is to put a spiritual magnifying glass to all that God is and declare these discoveries aloud.

The Greek word for magnify in Luke 1:46, *megaluno*, means "to make great." Nothing could provide so meaningful a conclusion to prayer as a statement of the greatness of God. With the psalmist we declare, "Great is the LORD, and greatly to be praised" (Ps. 48:1).

As prayer concludes we praise God because it has been His greatness that has made our devotional hour possible. When we began praying we recognized God's glory in all of its splendor and beauty. Now, we restate our case for worship. In these final moments we add faith to our praise. We actually praise God for future answers to prayer. With the psalmist we declare, "I will praise thee for ever, *because thou hast done it*" (Ps. 52:9, italics added).

Life's Highest Joy

Because every day must be lived in a spirit of praise, the specific practice of praise just before concluding prayer is essential. It prepares us for our highest function in life—to minister unto the Lord continuously.

Praise *in the closet* also prepares us to conquer our foes outside the closet. This truth is well supported by Paul Billheimer's testimony: "It [Praise] is the *summum bonum*, the greatest good, the highest joy, the most exquisite delight, the supreme rapture, and the most ravishing transport of the human spirit. Just as antagonism, hostility, and cursing against God exercises and strengthens all that is most abominable, diabolical, and base in the human spirit, so worship and praise of the infinitely loving, lovely God exercises, reinforces, and strengthens all that is most sublime, transcendent, and divine in the inner being. Thus as one worships and praises God, he is continually transformed step by step, from glory to glory into the image of the infinitely happy God."

Billheimer concludes, "Praise is the most useful occupation and activity in enabling God to realize the supreme goal of the universe, that of 'bringing many sons into glory.'"[1]

The bringing of lost souls to glory is the ultimate focal point for all prayer and praise. We *pray*, "Thy Kingdom come," and we *praise*, "For thine is the kingdom." Although much can be said about prayer, bringing glory to God is at the center of it. Professor Hallesby wrote, "The prayer life has its own laws, as all the rest of life has. The fundamental law in prayer is this: prayer is given and ordained for the purpose of glorifying God."[2]

When Jesus told His disciples, "Ye shall ask what ye will, and it shall be done unto you," He added, "Herein is my Father glorified" (John 15:7–8). God must be glorified through our praying, and praise enables the prayer warrior to keep this thought continually in focus.

The Attitude of Prayer

Perhaps the greatest secret to learn about prayer is how to maintain a devotional attitude after the devotional hour concludes. We must learn to take the spirit of praise with us from the prayer closet. No amount of prayer holds value if the prayer warrior remains unchanged. Said Andrew Murray, "Let us be careful to consider not only the length of the time we spend with God in prayer, but the power with which our prayer takes possession of our whole life."

The dedicated missionary concluded, "Learn this great lesson, my prayer must rule my whole life. What I request from prayer is not decided in five or ten minutes. I must learn to say: 'I have prayed with my whole heart.' What I desire from God must really fill my heart the whole day; then the way is open for a certain answer."[3]

Seize God's power during these closing moments of worship. Let an attitude of prayer flood your being as you prepare for your day. Always remember, God has been your power during prayer and will be your power throughout the day. Someone wisely suggested, "Spiritual power is not the power of prayer, but is the power of God realized in action through a man in the attitude of prayer."[4]

A Strong Amen

Jesus taught us to conclude our praying with the expression, "Amen" (Matt. 6:13). It means "so be it" or "it is done." A student of Greek told me that *amen* could actually be translated "God, our King, is trustworthy." To say "amen" in prayer is to express confidence that God has heard our petitions.

Martin Luther was known for his bold, almost brash petitioning of God. Yet Luther saw many dramatic answers to prayer. A friend once said of the reformation leader, "What a spirit, what a confidence was in his very expressions. With such a reverence he sued as one begging God, and yet with such hope and assurance, as if he spoke with a loving father or friend."[5]

It was Martin Luther who said of prayer's conclusion, "Mark this! Make your amen *strong*, never doubting that God is surely listening to you. This is what amen means: That I know with certainty that this prayer has been heard by God."

We, too, should end our praying with a strong expression of confidence. Paraphrase your "amen" with a testimony of faith. Say, "God, I know you can be trusted to bring these petitions into being. I confess my confidence in your promises. I praise you because it is done!"

The Gift of Praise

Thus, our sixty minutes with God has ended. We have not finished our praying with a list of personal petitions but with a spirit of grateful praise. When we leave the closet, we are not asking, but giving. Prayer has concluded with an offering of our lips. With the psalmist we have declared, "Accept, I beseech thee, the freewill offerings of my mouth" (Ps. 119:108).

Into a busy world we carry these words of divine magnification. Our goal beyond the closet is to magnify God's name in all we do. Every action will be sprinkled with silent worship. His praise shall be the very object of our conversation. The greatness of God shall dominate all thought and conduct. We leave the closet declaring with the poet:

Speak, lips of mine!
And tell abroad
The praises of my God.
Speak, stammering
   tongue!
In gladdest tone
Make His high praises
   known.

H. Bonar

Lord, teach me to magnify you!

Praise: The Twelfth Step in World-Changing Prayer

1. End your prayer with specific praise concerning God's greatness. Focus your praise on His omnipotence (power), His omniscience (knowledge), and His omnipresence (presence).
2. With the psalmist let us "praise God because He has done it." Look back at the devotional hour and praise God for hearing each of your requests.
3. Let your spirit "rejoice" for a few moments at the close of prayer. Repeat the universal word for praise, Hallelujah!
4. As Martin Luther suggested, when your devotional hour concludes make your "amen" strong. Confess with authority that you believe God is trustworthy.

14

The Destiny of Our Neighbors and Nations

Your Invitation to Be a "Watchman Warrior"

Now that we have a practical plan for prayer, we are faced with the matter of commitment. Am I willing to commit myself to give the Lord sixty minutes daily for prayer and Bible study? Would I also be willing to devote at least one of those hours during a week to be a part of a continuous "wall of prayer" for my community.

A unique biblical picture of a wall of prayer is found in Isaiah. We read: "O Jerusalem, I have posted watchmen on your walls; they will pray to the LORD day and night for the fulfillment of his promises. Take no rest, all you who pray. Give the LORD no rest until he makes Jerusalem the object of praise throughout the earth" (Isa. 62:6–7 NLT).

Across our nation and throughout the world (even China) believers are forming walls of prayer for their cities and towns. Because there are 168 hours in a week, a wall of prayer consists of at least one person covering each of those hours. Many churches are establishing walls of continuous prayer. Some communities have numerous churches cooperating to form multiple walls of prayer.

You can join such a wall, including Every Home for Christ's global wall of prayer for your neighbors and the nations by calling 1-800-423-5054, or by logging on to www.ehc.org, and clicking on the Wall of Prayer icon. A free kit will be sent to you that includes ideas for individuals, churches, and communities.

This book will help you and others stay faithful on the wall as well as help you develop your daily prayer life— even as much as an hour each day.

But commitment is the key! This personal commitment is of the utmost importance. Accomplishment always begins with a commitment of the will. To reach the peak of a mountain, a climber must first commit himself in the foothills. Once a commitment is made, follow-through and persistence are essential.

Concerning commitment in prayer, Professor Hallesby preached, "Certain requirements must be met if the art of prayer is to be acquired. In the main there are two: practice and perseverance. Without practice no Christian will become a real man or woman of prayer. And practice cannot be attained without perseverance."[1]

A faithful persistence is at the heart of a meaningful devotional habit. Andrew Murray, who said much concerning prayer's importance, also spoke about this quality in prayer. Discussing faithfulness, Murray said, "The Lord teaches us to know that the blessing through which we have so earnestly prayed can be preserved and increased in no other way than through intimate fellowship with Christ in the inner chamber, every day practiced and cultivated."[2]

This noted nineteenth-century missionary concluded, "Begin at the beginning. Be faithful in the inner chamber. Thank Him that you can reckon on Him to meet you there. Although everything appears cold, and dark, and restrained, bow in silence before the loving Lord Jesus, who so longs after you."[3]

Purposeful Regularity

Consistency is defined as "purposeful regularity." How do we develop purposeful regularity in the devotional habit?

First, *find the very best time for personal prayer*. Once you determine to develop a daily prayer habit, careful consideration should be given to *when* you pray. To discover your most effective time for prayer it may be necessary to do some experimenting.

Be careful not to rule out early morning prayer if you have never tried it. Set a goal of rising sixty to ninety minutes earlier than normal for at least several days of experimentation. You may be surprised to discover it is possible to function on less than your usual duration of sleep.

Seek also to set a *specific* time for prayer. Heed the warning, "Those who have no set time for prayer, do not pray."[4]

Recently I conducted a survey of twenty thousand prayer warriors who had pledged to pray sixty minutes daily. One question was directed specifically at those having difficulty keeping their commitment. Of those experiencing problems, the majority testified they set a goal to spend one hour daily with the Lord but never set a *specific* time to spend that hour.

Second, *declare your commitment verbally each day*. This is especially beneficial for the first several weeks of maintaining a daily prayer habit. State your commitment *vocally* upon arising each morning. Whether it is vocal or mental, it is of value to declare, "The most important appointment I have today is my appointment with Jesus in prayer." Other appointments or responsibilities may seem essential for the day, but nothing will approach the importance of intimate fellowship with the Lord.

Third, *fight all interruptions fiercely*. Paul spoke of fighting a "good fight" (1 Tim. 6:12). To believers at Ephesus he wrote, "Be ye angry. . . . Neither give place to the devil" (Eph. 4:26–27).

We must become angry at the satanic interruptions that seek to rob our day of prayer. Consistent, daily prayer often demands an all-out spiritual battle. Husbands and wives can assist one another in this regard. When I am in prayer my wife kindly tells visitors or callers that I am unable to be disturbed at that particular time. Such assistance proves of immeasurable help in conquering these interruptions.

Fourth, *develop a practical prayer plan.* Seek to establish prayer goals that provide incentives for entering the prayer closet. Using suggestions provided in previous chapters, develop a personal plan for prayer. Don't hesitate to vary the plan from day to day. Always invite the Holy Spirit to help you develop your program of prayer.

Finally, *recognize the overwhelming importance of your daily hour with God.* Until we recognize the full worth of our prayers, we will never develop a consistent habit of prayer. Years ago when I returned from an itinerary to the People's Republic of China, I carried as a reminder of my visit a copy of the small red book *Quotations from Mao Tse-tung.* Once home, I felt a deep conviction to hold this book daily in prayer, rebuking its power over the masses of China. I prayed that Mao's influence would deteriorate throughout Communist China.

Suddenly, newspapers and magazines seemed filled with articles discussing this very thing. As many as five unrelated articles reporting such changes appeared in one week just a few months after that trip.

Some might believe these events were a mere coincidence. I'm convinced prayer made the difference. Indeed, only as we become convinced that "believing" prayer truly changes things will we give ourselves to the daily exercise of prayer.

Results of Faithfulness

To be faithful in prayer is to share with God in His plan to change the world. Throughout every generation it has been the praying saint who has altered the course of history. Evangelist D. L. Moody reminded us, "Luther and his companions were men of such mighty pleading with God, that they broke the spell of ages, and laid nations subdued at the foot of the Cross. John Knox grasped all Scotland in his strong arms of faith and his prayers terrified tyrants. Whitefield, after much bold, faithful closet pleading, went to the devil's playground and took more than a thousand souls out of the jaws of the lion in one day."

With special anointing the evangelist added, "See a praying Wesley turn more than ten thousand souls to the Lord! Look at the praying Finney, whose prayers, faith, sermons and writings, have shaken this whole country and sent a wave of blessing through the churches on both sides of the sea."[5]

What happens when I am faithful to the closet of prayer? Not only do I reach out to help those who serve in the Lord's harvest around the world, but the impact of my personal prayer increases the very potential of my day. I soon find myself testifying with Dr. Payson, "Since I began to beg God's blessing on my studies, I have done more in one week than in a whole year before."[6]

Consider the influence of that eighteenth-century saint, David Brainerd. From a casual observation it would appear little was accomplished with his life. After all, Brainerd died at only twenty-nine years of age, having served only four years as an ordained minister. What could a struggling backwoods missionary possibly accomplish in just four years? Biographers tell us only forty or fifty persons were actually converted to Christ as the result of Brainerd's entire ministry.

Yet, something about Brainerd's devotional intensity affected generations of preachers. They were touched by his many days and nights of prayer in the frozen winter forests of northeastern America.

William Carey read Brainerd's journal and a divine flame ignited that reached across continents to touch the unevangelized of India. Edward Payson, John Wesley, Robert McCheyne, Andrew Murray, and Jonathan Edwards were but a few transformed by a mere contact with the written testimony of the young missionary.

Although he was almost twice the age of Brainerd, Jonathan Edwards—in whose home David Brainerd died—said after Brainerd's early death from tuberculosis, "I praise God that in His providence Brainerd should die in my house so that I might hear his prayers, so that I might witness his consecration, and be inspired by his example."[7]

The Destiny of Our Neighbors and Nations

Beloved, it is not age, experience, talent, or material wealth that makes the difference in the destiny of men and nations. Prayer alone will change the world, from our neighbors to the nations.

It is true that God may use age, experience, talent, and material wealth to help carry forth His purposes, but only when each is properly backed by prayer. Without prayer, every effort is wasted, for it leaves God out of the picture. Wise is the statement that there is much we can do *after* we have prayed but nothing we can do *until* we have prayed.

Thus, all of our questions are reduced to one: Will I say yes to the supreme plea of Jesus to watch with Him one hour? To say yes *today*, and every day, not only releases power into a neglected world, but it aligns me with the very ministry Jesus carries on *today*. Scripture says, "He ever liveth to make intercession" (Heb. 7:25).

Nothing I can do will please Christ more than my joining *with Him* in daily prayer. And when I do, something happens in the world, including my neighborhood, school, or workplace, that could not happen through any other means. My hour with Jesus, though brief in comparison to the ages of recorded time, actually makes a difference in the events that constitute these ages.

So, once again let our hearts stand silent as Jesus softly asks, "What, could you not watch with Me one hour?" It is a question each must answer, and on that answer hangs the destiny of my neighbors and the nations.

Lord, teach me to "always pray and not give up!" (Luke 18:1 NLT).

15

Final Thoughts

Scriptural Intercession and Practical Involvement

We know it is a good thing to pray for others, especially the millions living in unevangelized nations. But how can we be assured that our praying is truly scriptural?

Scriptural prayer for world evangelism basically centers in four areas. We might label these areas the "four claims" for world-changing prayer.

First, *claim workers for the harvest.* Daily in prayer I hold in my hands a special world prayer map prepared for concerned intercessors by Every Home for Christ.[1] Prior to my "making mention" of the various nations in prayer, I vocally claim each of these four scriptural items. I include the claim for workers first because Jesus included it first. Of all Christ taught in the Gospels, only once do we find Him sharing the ultimate solution to all problems of world evangelism.

Having painted the picture of a vast harvest, Jesus shares His only plan for reaping the harvest: "Therefore beseech the Lord of the harvest to send out workers into His harvest" (Matt. 9:38 NASB).

Nothing is more important in the worldwide work of God than those workers who shoulder the responsibilities of the harvest. God's plan centers in people. People who know

Jesus must share this knowledge with people who do not know Jesus. It is true that only God can give the "increase" (1 Cor. 3:6), but it is equally true that God will allow no increase without man's involvement. Augustine expressed it well, "Without God, we cannot, but without us, God will not!"[2]

Second, *claim open doors.* It is also scriptural to claim open doors for those workers who serve in the Lord's harvest. Indeed, the workers we claimed a moment ago will accomplish nothing if they have no field of labor. Even ten thousand qualified workers would accomplish very little in a nation where laws totally prohibit evangelistic activity. One third of the earth's population live under just such restrictions. This is why Paul told the Colossians, "Devote yourselves to prayer . . . that God may open up . . . a door for the word" (Col. 4:2–3 NASB).

To "devote" suggests we give ourselves earnestly to intercession for open doors of ministry. We should pray especially for specific leaders of nations who hold in their political hands the power to permit evangelistic outreach and church worship.

Paul told Timothy, "I exhort therefore, that, first of all, supplications, prayers, intercessions, and giving of thanks, be made for all men; For kings, and for all that are in authority" (1 Tim. 2:1–2).

Paul knew that evangelizing every nation is possible only if these leaders permit the peaceful spread of the gospel. Thus, he instructed us to pray for all those in authority.[3]

Third, *claim "fruit" that will remain.* Paul greatly desired that his efforts would not be in vain. "I desire fruit," he declared (Phil. 4:17). Of the Thessalonians Paul also requested, "Pray for us, that the word of the Lord may have free course, *and be glorified*" (2 Thess. 3:1, italics added). Paul longed that nothing would hinder the swift accomplishment of those goals God had given him. But more than that, he desired that every spiritual seed planted would take deep root.

Take time during prayer to lift those of Christ's body involved in caring for new converts. In many cultures a convert is rejected by both family and society. Without help the young believer finds it almost impossible to survive spiritually. Our prayers of intercession can actually make the difference.

Fourth, *claim a strong base of support for missionary outreach.* Until I traveled extensively overseas, I overlooked the importance of this claim. True, there is no specific Bible verse that says, "Pray that people will share more finances to help finish the task of world evangelism," but the Bible does stress the importance of sending forth workers. Of course, the sending forth of these workers bears a price tag.

After declaring that all who call upon the name of the Lord shall be saved, Paul stressed the need for workers to convey this message. Of Roman believers Paul asked, "How then shall they call on him in whom they have not believed? and how shall they believe in him of whom they have not heard? and how shall they hear without a preacher? And how shall they preach, *except they be sent?*" (Rom. 10:14–15, italics added).

The sending forth of workers, properly equipped with all the necessary tools, can be a very costly matter. Psalm 2:8 speaks of the lost being reached in the "uttermost parts" of the earth. Having spent many hours meditating on the difficult aspects of world evangelism, and traveling to remote places like Communist China, I am convinced that many Christians do not comprehend the enormous monetary responsibility in reaching these "uttermost parts."

For example, consider the thousands of islands that dot the world's oceans. Each must be visited by messengers of God's love. None can be overlooked. Jesus commissioned us to go into "all the world" (Mark 16:15).

But how costly and involved will this task be? Indonesia provides an excellent example. The fourth most populated country in the world, with 210 million people, Indonesia has a remarkable 17,000 separate islands (of which 3,000 are inhabited). After hearing this fact, one prayer warrior declared, "I suppose we should stop praying for God's army and start praying for God's navy."

Consider further that many islands include only a handful of inhabitants. In visiting both the Indonesian and Philippine island chains, Every Home for Christ workers have traveled entire days by boat to share printed gospel messages with only ten or twelve families *on a single island.* But until all are reached, the completion of the Great Commission is only a spiritual dream. To claim a strong base of support for evangelistic endeavor, and to become a part of that base, is to hasten the day of total world evangelization.

How to Pray for the Lost

Upon returning from the People's Republic of China in 1978, God deeply impressed our leadership to challenge prayer warriors to pray daily for a specific number of unevangelized Chinese. We began challenging intercessors to pray for 100 Chinese each day, asking that God would prepare their hearts for the message of salvation. An overall goal was set of mobilizing 300,000 such prayer warriors, each of whom would claim 100 Chinese daily, or 3,000 each month. Three hundred thousand praying in this manner would touch all 900 million Chinese at that time through prayer at least once every thirty days.

Although thousands initially accepted the challenge, and thousands more joined their ranks in the years that followed, the question quickly arose, "How do I pray for people I have never met, whose names I do not know, and yet pray for them intelligently *with purpose?*" The answer was discovered in prayer.

Because Jesus said, "Ask, and it shall be given" (Matt. 7:7), we must first believe that Christ will honor our simple faith whenever we request that He do something to prepare the hearts of lost souls. Whether praying for one hundred specific (though unknown) Chinese in a distant land, or an unsaved relative, we must believe something happens when we pray.

Of course, we do know that every person has a will to choose or reject the message of Christ's love. Therefore, we cannot ask God to force unbelievers, such as the one hundred specific Chinese, to believe on Him. In the first place, in the case of China and many other unevangelized nations, the vast majority of people have never heard about Jesus, so it is quite impossible for them to believe. It was this thought that led to a simple six-step plan to help Christians intercede for those they have never seen.

We recall from our elementary English classes the six interrogatives that introduce a question. They include who, what, when, why, how, and where. When praying for the lost, including my neighbors and those in distant nations, claim that God will cause these people to ask certain "heart" questions that will direct their thinking toward the things of God. This will prepare their hearts for the planting of gospel seeds.

Although this plan was originally developed to help intercessors focus prayer on groups of unevangelized Chinese, it can be adopted rather easily for the unsaved of any nation, or even for unconverted friends and family members.

Whom *Can I Trust?*

First, pray that lost souls will ask the question, *"Whom can I trust?"* Ask God to cause a specific person, or group of people, to begin questioning whom they can really trust in life. This is especially appropriate in repressed nations of the world. Pray that political leaders, such as the leaders of a particular Chinese province, will do certain things that will cause distrust throughout their province. When the people for whom we pray begin feeling this deep distrust they will wonder whom they can trust. Soon they will look for someone to trust beyond themselves. Eventually this search will direct their thinking heavenward!

What *Is My Purpose?*

Next, pray that lost souls will search for the meaning of life. Claim that each will inwardly ask, *"What is my purpose for living?"* This, too, will cause those for whom we intercede to contemplate the possibility of a Higher Power.

When *Will I Really Be Free?*

Then, pray that lost souls will ask, *"When will I really be free?"* This is especially appropriate for those living in Communist nations of the world, like China. Strangely, from a materialistic standpoint, the Chinese are far better off today than ever, especially when we compare current standards of living with those of thirty years ago. Thus, it is easy for the Chinese to be complacent and fail to realize how many personal freedoms have disappeared, including the right of Christians to freely worship or share the message of Christ.

Pray that God will plant in the hearts of these people, or other lost souls for whom you intercede, an inner unrest, together with a longing to know the "Truth" that will someday set them free.

Why *Do People Hate Religion?*

The fourth prayer interrogative concerns the question, *"Why do people hate religion?"* Although this request, like the others, is especially appropriate when praying for people of Communist nations, it can easily be adopted when praying for all who are without Christ. (For Muslims this question might be abbreviated to "Why do we hate?") Pray that lost souls will question why people find it necessary to fight the concept of God, especially if they don't believe in God anyway. (For Muslims we might ask God to fill their hearts with the question "Why is our religion so filled with hatred?")

Ultimately, this question will lead them on a deep "heart quest" that will create serious unresolved questions within them. Before long their desire to know the one true God will increase with great intensity.

How *Can I Cope?*

Next, pray that lost souls will ask, *"How can I cope with my problems?"* Pray that they will feel increasingly hopeless about personal problems, realizing that outside help must be found. This, too, will cause them to look for a Power beyond themselves.

Where *Will I Go when I Die?*

Finally, ask that lost souls will inwardly question, *"Where will I go when I die?"* This question may be asked by anyone. Even little children ask questions about death, especially when seeing a funeral procession or hearing that a relative has died. When interceding for lost souls, especially those we know very little about, we should pray that an urgency will fill their hearts concerning their eternal destination.

Imagine praying daily for a certain group of Chinese to inwardly ask the question, "Where will I go when I die?" Further imagine that those for whom you pray become obsessed with this question and even find themselves waking during the night and pondering these thoughts.

Then one day several of these Chinese receive a printed message of salvation in Christ and begin to read its message. Imagine their delight when they discover the promise, "For

God so loved the world, that he gave his only begotten Son, that whosoever believeth in him should not perish, but have everlasting life" (John 3:16).

This, beloved, is the power of specific, intercessory prayer when focused with compassion, with the aid of the Holy Spirit, on lost souls around the world.

And I can assure you, it works. Twenty-five years have passed since the challenge to pray the six interrogatives first appeared for China. At that time Every Home for Christ had no systematic evangelism campaign going on in China. As this 25th anniversary edition of *The Hour That Changes the World* is published, home-to-home evangelism has now touched all 800 of China's largest cities and has begun in over 1,000 of China's 1,676 towns of 25,000 to 100,000 people. In the 36 months leading up to this edition over 40 million families have been given the Gospel, home by home, in China. Clearly these prayers have made a difference.

Putting Feet to Our Prayers

But intercession is more than just praying for others. In my book *Love on its Knees* (Chosen Books, 1988), I wrote, "Intercession is far more a way of life than it is a type of prayer." At the heart of intercession is involvement in the very answers to the prayer we are praying.

Use Every Home for Christ's Lighthouse edition of its World Prayer Map to develop a plan to become a personal lighthouse by impacting both your neighbors and the nations. (Call EHC's toll free number 800-423-5054 or visit our web site at www.ehc.org to request a copy.)

Then, support missionary activity overseas through your local church or ministries like Every Home for Christ. (EHC's World Prayer Map mentioned above includes a wonderful way to help believers put feet to their prayers by reaching whole villages of previously unreached people, home by home, and hut by hut, with a personal presentation of the Gospel.)

Rees Howells, the extraordinary British intercessor during World War II perhaps sums these thoughts up best with his words: "You can never become a true intercessor until you are first willing to become a part of the answer to your own prayers."

Lord, teach me to get involved!

Notes

Chapter 1: *Prayer*

1. E. M Bounds, *The Necessity of Prayer*, quoted in *A Treasury of Prayer*, compiled by Leonard Ravenhill (Minneapolis: Bethany Fellowship, 1961), 30.

2. Charles H. Spurgeon, *Twelve Sermons on Prayer* (Grand Rapids: Baker Book House, 1971), 31.

3. Ibid., 36–70.

4. Helen Smith Shoemaker, *The Secret of Effective Prayer* (Waco, Tex.: Word Books, 1976), 15.

5. J. C. Ryle, *A Call to Prayer* (Grand Rapids: Baker Book House, 1976), 14–15.

6. David A. Hubbard, *The Problem with Prayer Is* (Wheaton, Ill.: Tyndale House Publishers, 1972), 51.

7. Bounds, *The Necessity of Prayer*, 184.

8. O. Hallesby, *Prayer* (Minneapolis: Augsburg Publishing House, 1959), 89.

9. Ibid., 88.

10. J. Oswald Sanders, *Prayer Power Unlimited* (Chicago: Moody Press, 1977), 108.

11. Harold Lindsell, *When You Pray* (Grand Rapids: Baker Book House, 1969), 25–26.

12. R. Humbard, *Praying with Power* (Grand Rapids: New Hope Press, 1975), 13.

13. Ryle, *A Call to Prayer*, 29–30.

Chapter 2: *Praise*

1. Brother Lawrence, *The Practice of the Presence of God* (Old Tappan, N.J.: Revell, 1959), 25.

2. Harold Lindsell, *When You Pray* (Grand Rapids: Baker Book House, 1975), 30–33.

3. Paul E. Billheimer, *Destined for the Throne* (Fort Washington, Pa.: Christian Literature Crusade, 1975), 118.

4. D. L. Moody, *Prevailing Prayer* (Chicago: Moody Press, n.d.), 55–56.

5. Billheimer, *Destined for the Throne*, 120.

Chapter 3: *Waiting*

1. E. M. Bounds, *The Weapon of Prayer* (Grand Rapids: Baker Book House, 1975), 156.

2. Bridgid E. Herman, *Creative Prayer* (New York: Harper and Row, n.d.), 31.

3. Edwin and Lillian Harvey, *Kneeling We Triumph* (Chicago: Moody Press, 1974), 66.

4. Ibid.

5. John Bisagno, *The Power of Positive Praying* (Grand Rapids: Zondervan, 1965), 70–72.

6. O. Hallesby, *Prayer* (Minneapolis: Augsburg Publishing House, 1959), 146.

7. Ibid., 147.

8. Norman Pittenger, *Praying Today* (Grand Rapids: Wm. B. Eerdmans, 1974), 35.

9. Harold Lindsell, *When You Pray* (Grand Rapids: Baker Book House, 1975), 31.

10. Donald E. Demaray, *Alive to God Through Prayer* (Grand Rapids: Baker Book House, 1956), 126–27.

11. Ralph Herring, *The Cycle of Prayer* (Wheaton, Ill.: Tyndale House Publishers, 1974), 16.

12. Herman, *Creative Prayer*, 40.

13. Harvey, *Kneeling We Triumph*, 73.

14. D. L. Moody, *Prevailing Prayer* (Chicago: Moody Press, n.d.), 18.

15. Andrew Murray, *The Prayer Life* (Chicago: Moody Press, n.d.), 43.

16. Herman, *Creative Prayer*, 33.

Chapter 4: *Confession*

1. Andrew Murray, *The Prayer Life* (Chicago: Moody Press, n.d.), 117.

2. D. L. Moody, *Prevailing Prayer* (Chicago: Moody Press, n.d.), 36–37.

3. William R. Parker and Elaine St. Johns, *Prayer Can Change Your Life* (Old Tappan, N.J.: Revell, 1975), 209.

4. E. M. Blaiklock, *The Positive Power of Prayer* (Glendale, Calif.: Regal, 1974), 43.

5. Harold Lindsell, *When You Pray* (Grand Rapids: Baker Book House, 1975), 37, 42.

6. Parker and St. Johns, *Prayer Can Change Your Life*, 220.

7. John Allan Lavender, *Why Prayers Are Unanswered* (Valley Forge, Pa.: Judson Press, 1967), 18.

8. Moody, *Prevailing Prayer*, 31–32.

9. Virginia Whitman, *The Excitement of Answered Prayer* (Grand Rapids: Baker Book House, 1978), 107.

10. Helen Smith Shoemaker, *The Secret of Effective Prayer* (Waco, Tex.: Word Books, 1967), 64.

11. David A. Hubbard, *The Problem with Prayer Is* (Wheaton, Ill.: Tyndale House Publishers, 1972), 74.

Chapter 5: *Scripture Praying*

1. Leonard Ravenhill, *Why Revival Tarries* (Minneapolis: Bethany Fellowship, 1959), 59.

2. E. M. Bounds, *The Necessity of Prayer* (Grand Rapids: Baker Book House, 1976), 10.

3. E. W. Kenyon, *In His Presence* (Lynnwood, Wa.: Gospel Publishing Society, 1969), 32.

4. Andrew Murray, *The Prayer Life* (Chicago: Moody Press, n.d.), 107.

5. Lehman Strauss, *Sense and Nonsense About Prayer* (Chicago: Moody Press, 1974), 65–66.

6. G. Campbell Morgan, *The Practice of Prayer* (Grand Rapids: Baker Book House, 1971), 95.

7. George Mueller, *An Autobiography of George Mueller* (London: J. Nisbet, 1906), 150.

8. E. M. Bounds, *The Possibilities of Prayer* (Minneapolis: Bethany Fellowship, 1978).

9. Jack R. Taylor, *Prayer: Life's Limitless Reach* (Nashville: Broadman Press, 1977), 109.

10. J. Oswald Sanders, *Prayer Power Unlimited* (Chicago: Moody Press, 1977), 9.

Chapter 6: *Watching*

1. Jack R. Taylor, *Prayer: Life's Limitless Reach* (Nashville: Broadman Press, 1977), 111.

2. Curtis C. Mitchell, *Praying Jesus' Way* (Old Tappan, N.J.: Revell, 1977), 79–80.

3. Watchman Nee, *The Prayer Ministry of the Church* (New York: Christian Fellowship Publishers, 1973), 121.

4. Christians interested in monthly "prayer fuel" that will aid them in "watching" the needs of world evangelism may write to Every Home for Christ, P.O. Box 64000, Colorado Springs, CO 80962.

5. J. C. Ryle, *A Call to Prayer* (Grand Rapids: Baker Book House, 1976), 59.

6. Ibid., 60.

7. Lehman Strauss, *Sense and Nonsense About Prayer* (Chicago: Moody Press, 1974), 31.

8. Donald E. Demaray, *Alive to God Through Prayer* (Grand Rapids: Baker Book House, 1965), 81.

9. Taylor, *Prayer: Life's Limitless Reach*, 75.

10. O. Hallesby, *Prayer* (Minneapolis: Augsburg Publishing House, 1959), 169–70.

11. Anne J. Townsend, *Prayer Without Pretending* (Chicago: Moody Press, 1973), 95.

12. Andrew Murray, *The Prayer Life* (Chicago: Moody Press, n.d.), 64–65.

Chapter 7: *Intercession*

1. Paul E. Billheimer, *Destined for the Throne* (Fort Washington, Pa.: Christian Literature Crusade, 1975), 19.

2. William L. Krutza, *How Much Prayer Should a Hamburger Get?* (Grand Rapids: Baker Book House, 1975), 21.

3. Billheimer, *Destined for the Throne*, 105.

4. E. M Bounds, *The Weapon of Prayer* (Grand Rapids: Baker Book House, 1975), 58.

5. Some readers may wonder why two common prayer terms—*travail* and *supplication*—are not listed in our discussion as specific elements of the devotional habit. *Travail* is an intense form of intercession, whereas *supplication* is an intense form of petition. Thus, to plead with great intensity for a personal need is a type of petition called *supplication*. To plead with great intensity for the needs of another is a type of intercessory prayer called *travail*. The author's earlier book on prayer, *No Easy Road: Inspirational Thoughts on Prayer* (Grand Rapids: Baker Book House, 1971), presents a look at both supplication and travail in relationship to prayer.

6. Edwin and Lillian Harvey, *Kneeling We Triumph* (Chicago: Moody Press, 1974), 40.

7. Ibid., 98.

8. Anne J. Townsend, *Prayer Without Pretending* (Chicago: Moody Press, 1973), 82.

9. J. C. Ryle, *A Call to Prayer* (Grand Rapids: Baker Book House, 1976), 73.

10. Bounds, *The Weapon of Prayer*, 70.

11. Jack R. Taylor, *Prayer: Life's Limitless Reach* (Nashville: Broadman Press, 1977), 75.

12. The apostle Paul also referred to "making mention" of fellow workers in prayer in Eph. 1:16, Phil. 1:3–4, and 1 Thess. 1:2.

13. R. E. Speer, *Paul, The All-Round Man* (New York: Revell, 1909), 92.

14. O. Hallesby, *Prayer* (Minneapolis: Augsburg Publishing House, 1959), 164–65.

Chapter 8: *Petition*

1. Helen Smith Shoemaker, *The Secret of Effective Prayer* (Waco, Tex.: Word Books, 1967), 51.

2. Charles H. Spurgeon, *Twelve Sermons on Prayer* (Grand Rapids: Baker Book House, 1971), 99.

3. E. M. Bounds, *The Weapon of Prayer* (Grand Rapids: Baker Book House, 1975), 106.

4. E. M. Blaiklock, *The Positive Power of Prayer* (Glendale, Calif.: Regal, 1974), 35–37.

5. Spurgeon, *Twelve Sermons on Prayer*, 38.

6. Andrew Murray, *The Prayer Life* (Chicago: Moody Press, n.d.), 95.

7. D. L. Moody, *Prevailing Prayer* (Chicago: Moody Press, n.d.), 18.

8. Murray, *The Prayer Life*, 96.

Chapter 9: *Thanksgiving*

1. O. Hallesby, *Prayer* (Minneapolis: Augsburg Publishing House, 1959), 141.

Chapter 10: *Singing*

1. Donald E. Demaray, *Alive to God Through Prayer* (Grand Rapids: Baker Book House, 1965), 27.

2. A full color map of all the nations with indexed locations is available upon request from Every Home for Christ, P.O. Box 64000, Colorado Springs, CO 80962.

Chapter 11: *Meditation*

1. Bridgid E. Herman, *Creative Prayer* (New York: Harper and Row, n.d.), 48–49.

2. E. M. Blaiklock, *The Positive Power of Prayer* (Glendale, Calif.: Regal, 1974), 38–39.

3. Herman, *Creative Prayer*, 55.

4. Ibid., 60–66.

5. Ibid., 47.

6. Ibid., 53.

7. Brother Lawrence, *The Practice of the Presence of God* (Old Tappan, N.J.: Revell, 1958), 11–12.

Chapter 12: *Listening*

1. Bridgid E. Herman, *Christian Prayer* (New York: Harper and Row, n.d.), 25.

2. Rosalind Rinker, *Prayer: Conversing with God* (Grand Rapids: Zondervan, 1959), 17–18.

3. Hope MacDonald, *Discovering How to Pray* (Grand Rapids: Zondervan, 1976), 53–54.

4. Edwin and Lillian Harvey, *Kneeling We Triumph* (Chicago: Moody Press, 1974), 81.

5. Ibid., 78.

6. David A. Hubbard, *The Problem with Prayer Is* (Wheaton, Ill.: Tyndale House Publishers, 1972), 51.

7. Donald E. Demaray, *Alive to God Through Prayer* (Grand Rapids: Baker Book House, 1965), 41.

8. John Anthony Hanne, *Prayer or Pretense* (Grand Rapids: Zondervan, 1974), 22–23.

9. Herman, *Creative Prayer*, 43.

10. Harvey, *Kneeling We Triumph*, 81.

11. Herman, *Creative Prayer*, 43.

Chapter 13: *Praise*

1. Paul E. Billheimer, *Destined for the Throne* (Fort Washington, Pa.: Christian Literature Crusade, 1957), 117.

2. O. Hallesby, *Prayer* (Minneapolis: Augsburg Publishing House, 1959), 126.

3. Andrew Murray, *The Prayer Life* (Chicago: Moody Press, n.d.), 118.

4. John Anthony Hanne, *Prayer or Pretense* (Grand Rapids: Zondervan, 1974), 48.

5. J. C. Ryle, *A Call to Prayer* (Grand Rapids: Baker Book House, 1976), 68.

Chapter 14: *The Destiny of Our Neighbors and Nations*

1. O. Hallesby, *Prayer* (Minneapolis: Augsburg Publishing House, 1959), 40.

2. Andrew Murray, *The Prayer Life* (Chicago: Moody Press, n.d.), 134.

3. Ibid., 147.

4. Watchman Nee, *The Prayer Ministry of the Church* (New York: Christian Fellowship Publishers, 1973), 114.

5. D. L. Moody, *Prevailing Prayer* (Chicago: Moody Press, n.d.), 16.

6. Ibid., 14.

7. *The Life of Reverend David Brainerd*, consisting of David Brainerd's memoirs and personal journal, has been recently reprinted by Baker Book House, Grand Rapids, MI 49516, after being out of print for almost two decades.

Chapter 15: *Final Thoughts*

1. A map of the world, listing all the nations of the world and showing their locations, is available upon request from Every Home for Christ, P.O. Box 64000, Colorado Springs, CO 80962.

2. Norman Pittenger, *Praying Today* (Grand Rapids: Wm. B. Eerdmans, 1974), 152.

3. Every Home for Christ's World Prayer Map also includes a list of all the heads of state for each nation so intercessors can pray intelligently for those in authority (1 Tim. 2:1–2).

Because prayer is a subject that touches every generation, the Church has been blessed with a legacy of written dialogue on prayer themes from scores of godly authors. In presenting a specific plan for daily systematic prayer, *The Hour That Changes the World* features insights from many of these authors. The bibliography on page 145 not only lists those authors quoted directly in this work, but also includes books that have influenced me in preparing these pages. I am deeply grateful to the many publishers who have granted permission to quote these outstanding teachers of prayer.

Bibliography

Allen, Charles L. *All Things Are Possible Through Prayer*. Old Tappan, N.J.: Revell, 1958.

Billheimer, Paul E. *Destined for the Throne*. Fort Washington, Pa.: Christian Literature Crusade, 1975.

Bisagno, John. *The Power of Positive Praying*. Grand Rapids: Zondervan, 1965.

Blaiklock, E. M. *The Positive Power of Prayer*. Glendale, Calif.: Regal, 1974.

Bounds, E. M. *The Essentials of Prayer*. Minneapolis: Bethany Fellowship, 1976.

———. *The Necessity of Prayer*. Grand Rapids: Baker Book House, 1976.

———. *The Possibilities of Prayer*. Minneapolis: Bethany Fellowship, 1978.

———. *Prayer and Praying Men*. Grand Rapids: Baker Book House, 1977.

———. *Purpose in Prayer*. Grand Rapids: Baker Book House, 1978.

———. *The Reality of Prayer*. Grand Rapids: Baker Book House, 1978.

———. *The Weapon of Prayer*. Grand Rapids: Baker Book House, 1975.

Bunyan, John. *Prayer*. London: Banner of Truth Trust, 1965.

Chadwick, Samuel. *The Path of Prayer*. Fort Washington, Pa.: Christian Literature Crusade, 1963.

Christenson, Evelyn, and Viola Blake. *What Happens When Women Pray*. Wheaton, Ill.: Victor Books, 1976.

Demaray, Donald E. *Alive to God Through Prayer*. Grand Rapids: Baker Book House, 1965.

Eastman, Dick. *No Easy Road*. Grand Rapids: Baker Book House, 1971.

———. *Love On Its Knees*. Old Tappan, N.J.: Chosen, 1989.

———. *Dick Eastman on Prayer*. Grand Rapids: Global Christian Publishers, 1999.

Edwards, Jonathan. *The Life of Reverend David Brainerd*. Grand Rapids: Baker Book House, 1978.

Finney, Charles G. *Prevailing Prayer*. Grand Rapids: Kregel, 1965.

Gesswein, Armin R. *Seven Wonders of Prayer*. Grand Rapids: Zondervan, 1957.

Goforth, Rosalind. *How I Know God Answers Prayer*. Chicago: Moody Press, n.d.

Gordon, Samuel D. *Quiet Talks on Prayer*. New York: Grosset and Dunlap, 1904.

Grubb, Norman P. *Rees Howells: Intercessor*. Fort Washington, Pa.: Christian Literature Crusade, 1962.

Hallesby, O. *Prayer*. Minneapolis: Augsburg Publishing House, 1959.

Hanne, John Anthony. *Prayer or Pretense?* Grand Rapids: Zondervan, 1974.

Harvey, Edwin and Lillian. *Kneeling We Triumph*. Chicago: Moody Press, 1974.

Hasler, Richard. *Journey with David Brainerd*. Downers Grove, Ill.: InterVarsity Press, 1976.

Hayford, Jack W. *Prayer Is Invading the Impossible*. Plainfield, N.J.: Logos International, 1977.

Herman, Bridgid E. *Creative Prayer*. Cincinnati: Forward Movement Publications, n.d.

Herring, Ralph. *The Cycle of Prayer*. Wheaton, Ill.: Tyndale House Publishers, 1974.

Hubbard, David A. *The Problem with Prayer Is*. Wheaton, Ill.: Tyndale House Publishers, 1972.

Huegel, F. J. *The Ministry of Intercession*. Minneapolis: Bethany Fellowship, 1967.

————. *Prayer's Deeper Secrets*. Grand Rapids: Zondervan, 1959.

————. *Successful Praying*. Minneapolis: Bethany Fellowship, 1967.

Humbard, Rex. *Praying with Power*. Grand Rapids: New Hope Press, 1975.

Kenyon, E. W. *In His Presence*. Lynnwood, Wa.: Gospel Publishing Society, 1969.

Kimmel, Jo. *Steps to Prayer Power*. Nashville: Abingdon Press, 1972.

The Kneeling Christian. Grand Rapids: Zondervan, 1945.

Lauback, Frank C. *Prayer, the Mightiest Force in the World*. Old Tappan, N.J.: Revell, 1959.

Lavender, John Allan. *Why Prayers Are Unanswered*. Valley Forge, Pa.: Judson Press, 1967.

Lawrence, Brother. *Practice of the Presence of God*. Old Tappan, N.J.: Revell, 1956.

Lawson, Gilchrist. *Deeper Experiences of Famous Christians*. Anderson, Ind.: Warner Press, 1911.

Lindsell, Harold. *When You Pray*. Grand Rapids: Baker Book House, 1975.

McClure, J. G. *Intercessory Prayer*. Chicago: Moody Press, n.d.

McDonald, Hope. *Discovering How to Pray*. Grand Rapids: Zondervan, 1976.

McGraw, Francis A. *Praying Hyde*. Chicago: Moody Press, n.d.

Moody, D. L. *Prevailing Prayer*. Chicago: Moody Press, n.d.

Morgan, G. Campbell. *The Practice of Prayer*. Grand Rapids: Baker Book House, 1971.

Mueller, George. *Answers to Prayer*. Chicago: Moody Press, n.d.

Murray, Andrew. *The Prayer Life*. Chicago: Moody Press, n.d.

————. *With Christ in the School of Prayer*. Old Tappan, N.J.: Revell, 1953.

Parker, William, R., and Elaine St. Johns. *Prayer Can Change Your Life*. Old Tappan, N.J.: Revell, 1975.

Payne, Thomas. *Prayer—The Greatest Force on Earth*. Chicago: Moody Press, n.d.

Pittenger, Norman. *Praying Today*. Grand Rapids: Wm. B. Eerdmans, 1974.

Prater, Arnold. *You Can Pray as You Ought*. Nashville: Nelson, 1977.

Ravenhill, Leonard. *Why Revival Tarries*. Minneapolis: Bethany Fellowship, 1959.

Redpath, Alan. *Victorious Praying*. Old Tappan, N.J.: Revell, 1957.

Reidhead, Paris. *Beyond Petition*. Minneapolis: Bethany Fellowship, 1974.

Rinker, Rosalind. *Prayer: Conversing with God*. Grand Rapids: Zondervan, 1959.

Ryle, J. C. *A Call to Prayer*. Grand Rapids: Baker Book House, 1976.

Sanders, J. Oswald. *Prayer Power Unlimited*. Minneapolis: World Wide Publications, 1977.

Sheen, Fulton J. *Life of Christ*. Garden City, N.Y.: Image Books, 1977.

Shoemaker, Helen Smith. *The Secret of Effective Prayer*. Waco, Tex.: Word Books, 1967.

Sims, A. *George Mueller: Man of Faith*. Chicago: Moody Press, n.d.

Spurgeon Charles H. *Effective Prayer*. London: Evangelical Press, n.d.

————. *Twelve Sermons on Prayer*. Grand Rapids: Baker Book House, 1971.

Stedman, Ray C. *Jesus Teaches on Prayer*. Waco, Tex.: Word Books, 1976.

Steere, Douglas V. *Dimensions of Prayer*. New York: Harper and Row, 1963.

Strauss, Lehman. *Sense and Nonsense About Prayers*. Chicago: Moody Press, 1976.

Taylor, Jack R. *Prayer: Life's Limitless Reach*. Nashville: Broadman Press, 1977.

Thielicke, Helmut. *Our Heavenly Father*. Grand Rapids: Baker Book House, 1974.

Torrey, R. A. *The Power of Prayer*. Grand Rapids: Zondervan, 1974.

Townsend, Anne J. *Prayer Without Pretending*. Chicago: Moody Press, 1976.

Tozer, A. W. *The Knowledge of the Holy*. New York: Harper and Row, 1975.

Wallis, Arthur. *Jesus Prayed*. Fort Washington, Pa.: Christian Literature Crusade, 1966.

Whyte, Alexander. *Lord, Teach Us to Pray*. Grand Rapids: Baker Book House, 1976.

Dick Eastman is president of Every Home for Christ and originator of the Change the World School of Prayer. He has also written *A Celebration of Praise* and *No Easy Road*, with more than 600,000 copies in print.

Every Home for Christ . . .
Reaching the Nations One Family at a Time!

EVERY HOME FOR CHRIST, led by Dr. Dick Eastman,
author of *The Hour That Changes the World,* is a global
home-to-home evangelism ministry (formerly known as
World Literature Crusade) that has worked with more than
500 denominations and mission organizations to conduct
Every Home Campaigns in 190 nations.

Since its inception, Every Home for Christ, with a full-
time staff of over 1,200 workers plus over 2,400 volunteer
associates, has distributed over 2.1 billion gospel messages
home by home, resulting in over 27.5 million decision
cards being mailed to EHC's numerous offices overseas and
the establishment of over 43,000 village New Testament
fellowships called "Christ Groups." Where illiterate people
groups exist, EHC distributes gospel records and
audiotapes, including the amazing "card talks" (cardboard
record players). In one recent 12-month period 1,485,284
decision cards were received in EHC offices around the
world, or an average of 4,069 *every day!*

To date, Every Home Campaigns have been conducted in
190 countries and completed in 90. The EHC ministry
presently maintains 100 offices throughout the world,
including campaigns in much of the former Soviet Union
and all 32 provinces and autonomous regions of China.

Because some areas of the world are virtually closed to Christian outreach, particularly in Middle Eastern countries, Every Home for Christ has developed an especially strong prayer mobilization effort through its multi-hour *Change the World School of Prayer* originated by Dick Eastman. More than 2,000,000 Christians in 120 nations have been impacted by this training, por-tions of which are now on DVD (video) in over 50 languages.

EHC's *Feed 5000* campaign enables believers to reach at least 5,000 people with the Gospel, over the course of a year. *Feed 5000* gives individuals a way to put feet to their prayers for the lost by providing gospel booklets and Bible-study materials that present Jesus, "the Bread of Life," for families who need to discover His offer of salvation.

Dick Eastman invites you to learn more about this oppor-tunity by contacting Every Home for Christ for a full-color Lighthouse Edition of EHC's World Prayer Map which includes information about how to become involved in feeding 5,000 the Bread of Life annually.

In the USA: Call toll-free 1-800-423-5054
Also, in the USA: 1-719-260-8888
P.O. Box 64000, Colorado Springs, CO 80962
In Canada: 1-800-265-7326
P.O. Box 3636, Guelph, Ontario, Canada N1H 7S2
For other global addresses, contact EHC in the USA.
Visit our web site at www.ehc.org

Editor's information on Joni Eareckson Tada

The week before she packed her bags for college back in 1967, Joni Eareckson went swimming in the Chesapeake Bay with her sister. It was one visit to the beach that would change her life. A diving accident that day left her paralyzed from the shoulders down. After two years of rehabilitation, Joni rose out of depression through the help and support of Christian friends. She went on to become an accomplished author and artist, writing more than 25 books.

Joni eventually moved to southern California, where she established Joni and Friends, a nonprofit ministry that promotes the love of Christ among families affected by disability. In 1982 Joni married Ken Tada. They presently reside in Calabasas, California.

Joni has served as a national disability advocate and was appointed by Presidents Reagan and Bush to the National Council on Disability. During her tenure the Americans with Disabilities Act was drafted and became law.

Joni and Ken devote much time to the programs at Joni and Friends, which include Wheels for the World, an outreach that refurbishes used but serviceable wheelchairs and fits them to people with disabilities in developing nations.

For more information on how your church can start a disability outreach, contact Joni and Friends at P.O. Box 3333, Agoura Hills, CA 91301 or www.joniandfriends.org.

CHANGE THE WORLD...
From your neighbors to the nations

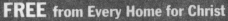

You Can Spread the Vision of
The Hour That Changes the World . . .

Through Dick Eastman's exciting 13-lesson video training course

PRACTICAL PRAYER . . .
A fast-paced, 13-lesson video series based on Dick Eastman's best-selling book *The Hour That Changes the World.* Ideal for cell groups, Sunday school classes, prayer groups, and even home schoolers 12 years and above.

Available from Every Home for Christ. See information below.

Other books available by the author of *The Hour That Changes the World* . . .

Beyond Imagination:
A Simple Plan to Save
the World

Dick Eastman's new "delight trilogy" on intercessory worship: *Heights of Delight, Pathways of Delight* and *Rivers of Delight.*